Murder & Crime

KINGSTON-UPON-HULL

Murder & Crime

KINGSTON-UPON-HULL

DOUGLAS WYNN

The History Press

First published in 2008

The History Press
The Mill, Brimscombe Port,
Stroud, Gloucestershire, GL5 2QG
www.thehistorypress.co.uk

Reprinted in 2008, 2010

British Library Cataloguing in Publication Data.
A catalogue record for this book is available from the British Library.

ISBN 978 0 7524 4662 2

Typesetting and origination by
The History Press
Printed in Great Britain

Contents

Acknowledgements   6

Introduction   7

1   Killer Conman   11

2   'My Girl must not be Involved'   19

3   Murder at the Institution   25

4   Lucky Murderer   31

5   Sins of the Son   40

6   The Power of Dreams   46

7   Calypso Killer   55

8   'My God! What has he been doing to you?'   60

9   She Committed Murder when she was Dead   68

10 A Day at the Races   74

11 The Best Lain Schemes o' Mice an' Women   81

12 A Private War   89

    Bibliography   95

Acknowledgements

Many people have helped me with this book and if I haven't thanked them all please forgive me and take the thanks as understood. I should particularly like to thank David Smith, senior local studies librarian, and his staff at the Hull Central Library for their kindness, forbearance and unstinting assistance; also Jason Morris at the Grimsby Central Library, for a great deal of help with illustrations. Simon Drury of Memory Lane was very helpful, and without him and John Markham I should not have been able to contact Ian Samuel and Andrew Sefton of Pocklington, who went out of their way to help me. I should also like to thank Margaret Tinkler for the loan of books and David N. Robinson for helpful discussions. I should particularly like to thank Cate Ludlow of The History Press Ltd for all her help and encouragement during the writing of this book. I am also grateful to the editor of the *Hull Daily Mail* for permission to reproduce material from his newspapers and to the editor of the *Grimsby Telegraph* for permission to reproduce photographs from his collection; also to the Associated Newspapers Ltd for permission to reproduce part of the *Daily Sketch*. And as ever my grateful thanks to Rosemary for help with the research and with the driving and being a constant support: without her this book would not have been possible.

Introduction

An entry in the Domesday Book of 1086 mentions Myton, describing it as a farm at the confluence of two rivers, presumably the River Hull and the Humber. It was around about this time that the monks from Meaux Abbey established a port at Wyke, called Wyke upon Hull. It soon became the most flourishing port in the north of England and wool was collected there before being shipped to France to pay for the ransom of King Richard I. One hundred years later Edward I needed a fortified port in the north for supplying his armies fighting the Scots. He therefore bought Wyke from the monks, laid out a new town with fortifications and called it Kyngestone upon Hull. At that time the port traded in wine, wool, coal, iron, timber, cloth and corn. It received its Royal Charter making it a borough in 1299 and it then had its own coroner, a prison and a gallows. Soon after this a mint was established there.

Edward II replaced the wooden defences with brick walls circling the town, which was on the west side of the River Hull: they went from the bank of the Hull to the Humber. There was a moat, thirty towers and four main gates with portcullises, and to stop enemy ships going up the Hull a chain was placed across its mouth. Henry VIII was another King who improved the town's defences because of the rebellion in Lincolnshire and Yorkshire known as the Pilgrimage of Grace. And when there were fears of a Spanish invasion in 1626, they were updated yet again by Charles I.

Charles visited the town himself in 1639 and was received cordially. But relations between the King and Parliament were deteriorating fast, and in 1642 he moved his court from London to York. A civil war was inevitable and the port of Kingston-upon-Hull would help to supply Charles's armies. He decided to secure the port by a trick. In April he sent his son, the Duke of York and future James II, to the town on a goodwill visit. The duke was entertained by the mayor and put up overnight. The next day while he was being shown around he produced a letter saying that the King was on his way to Hull. The governor of the town, Sir John Hotham, who had been recently appointed by Parliament, conferred with other dignitaries and they agreed to deny the King access to the town: when Charles arrived at the Beverley Gate with a force of 300 soldiers he found the drawbridge up against him. He threatened and cajoled, but admittance was refused and eventually he left with his son. Later that year the town came under siege from Royalist forces, but it did not fall. It survived another siege during the war and was the only important town in Yorkshire not to be occupied by Royalist troops.

By the eighteenth century the town and port had become so prosperous that its population increased and residents began building houses outside the walls. William Wilberforce, who was largely responsible for getting the bill banning slavery through Parliament, was born in Hull in 1759, it is said in a house which King Charles I had stayed in on one of his visits. Kingston-upon-Hull finally became a city in 1897.

Apart from being one of the most important ports on the East Coast, Hull was also one of the leading ports in the whaling industry. Whaling had been carried out by many European nations – including the Norwegians, the French, the Spanish and latterly the Dutch – from as early as the eighth and ninth centuries. But it was only in the 1750s that ships from Hull started whaling. Many types of whales were hunted, including the sperm whale, the white whale, the narwhale and the common, or Greenland, whale. Their blubber was rendered down for the oil, which was used in lighting – both domestic and street lighting – and also in making soap, paint and in curing leather. Whalebone had a number of uses, including stiffening women's corsets, and ambergris was used in perfumes and jewellery.

The Hull whalers carried a crew of thirty to fifty men and boys and, apart from the captain, had a surgeon and various specialised trades including harpooners, carpenters and coopers. Trips lasted anything up to four to five months and it usually took three weeks or more to get to the hunting grounds in the Arctic Ocean, around Greenland or north of Norway. The Hull ships were very successful and by 1790 the port vied with London as the premier whaling centre in England. By 1830 sixty-five whalers were based in Hull. But the industry had a short life. Dwindling numbers of whales and the declining demand for whale oil (it was largely replaced by coal gas) meant that by the 1850s there were very few ships leaving Hull for the whaling grounds.

But as one seafaring industry was ending another was beginning to expand. Fishing had been followed in the Humber and in the North Sea since time immemorial, but it was the discovery in 1843 of the Dogger Bank in the North Sea, with its vast stocks of fish, and the coming of the railways to the north bank of the Humber, that fuelled a dramatic expansion. In 1863 Hull had 270 fishing smacks, most of them crowded into a corner of the Humber Dock, but by 1869 they were accommodated in the newly built Albert Dock running alongside the Humber itself. Ten years later there were 420 smacks and ice was now being used to keep the fish fresh on board. The 1880s also saw the expansion of the fishing fleets, where fast cutters unloaded the fish from the smacks while they were still at sea and took the catches back to port. In 1883 the St Andrews Dock was built, extending the facilities even further west along the Humber Bank. And this led to the formation of close-knit fishing communities which grew up along the Hessle road.

Fishing was a hard life, especially for the apprentice boys. They could be anywhere from twelve to twenty-one years old and were often drawn from orphan homes and other institutions. They were poorly fed and clothed and frequently had nowhere to live between voyages. Fourteen-year-old William Pepper (or Papper, as he is sometimes called) was better off than most boys; he was apprenticed to Otto Brand (twenty-seven), who was the skipper and part owner of the fishing smack the *Rising Sun* and he lived with him in between voyages instead of his own family.

The *Rising Sun* left for the North Sea fishing grounds on a very cold day on 16 December 1881. But before they left Pepper passed a remark to his skipper that he thought the skipper knew his sister. Brand took exception to this and shouted at the boy. The remark seems to have festered in his mind and before the smack had reached Spurn he was already subjecting the boy to physical abuse. He threw buckets of freezing sea water over the lad and beat him with the knotted end of a rope. When they were out in the North Sea the beating continued and anything that went wrong with the ship and its gear, like a hole appearing in the nets, he blamed on the youngster. At one stage he put a rope round his neck and nearly throttled him – he then tied him to the ship's rail and threw buckets of water over him. While the rest of the crew fed well, Pepper was starved with broken biscuits and water. Brand also encouraged the crew to abuse the boy and wouldn't allow him to have any Christmas dinner. The beatings became more savage and on 29 December Pepper was found lying on the deck unconscious by one of the crew.

The crew member reported to the skipper that he could not revive the boy and feared he was dead. Brand replied that they could not take the boy back to Hull since his face was so disfigured by the beating. They wrapped him in sailcloth and threw him overboard. When they reached port Brand claimed that the boy had fallen in the sea and drowned. But the crew, even though they had themselves abused Pepper, were so appalled at the skipper's conduct that they gave evidence against him. He was tried for murder, convicted and hanged at Leeds Prison on 22 May 1882.

In that same year another fisherman, Edward Wheatfield, a mate on a fishing smack, physically abused Peter Hughes, another apprentice, until he too died. Wheatfield was also convicted of murder and hanged in Leeds.

There are many more murders in this book, from the man who buried not one but two of his families under the kitchen floor and the murderer who was discovered by a mother's dream to the man who got away with murder three times and the woman who committed a murder after she was dead.

Serial killer Frederick Bailey Deeming, alias Albert Williams.

Marie Deeming, who was murdered at Rainhill.

I

Killer Conman

'Albert,' she said, 'I don't know that I ought to be going into a strange house alone with you. We are not married and I haven't a chaperone with me.'

'My dear Emily, I am a perfectly respectable inspector of regiments.'

Albert Williams, who was in his forties, was a small fair-haired man, with the luxurious moustache that most men wore in the 1890s. And he curled it and threw out his chest as if to make himself look more important. Emily giggled. She was in her early twenties. 'You never did tell me what an inspector of regiments is. But I'm sure it's very important.'

'Of course it is. But it's not a regular rank. I'm a civilian really, but I advise the Army on tunnelling and such like. I'm a mining engineer really.'

'But you do have a uniform. I've seen it.'

'Yes, but that's just for ceremonial occasions. Now come on if I'm going to show you round this house. I've leased it at the behest of my good friend Colonel Brooks. He's at the War Office, but he's very fussy and wanted all sorts of alterations done before he moved in. As you know I've only been in Rainhill a few months.'

'I remember when you first came into my mother's shop to buy your paper.' Albert looked down at her fondly. 'Emily Mather. You are romantic!'

'Well why not? We are walking out aren't we?'

'Of course we are, and now we are going to walk up this path and I am going to show you round this house.' Together they trudged up the overgrown path of Denham Villa, Lawton Road, Rainhill, which was a small town on the outskirts of Liverpool between the city and St Helens, Lancashire. He showed Emily round the house and they finished up in the kitchen. By this time Emily was rather tired and when Albert drew her attention to the new concrete floor which he had laid, she was less than enthusiastic. 'Can we go now Albert? I'm getting a little fatigued.'

'Of course we can. But before we go I have an important thing to say to you.'

'Oh yes?' said Emily, suddenly brightening up and looking up at him with expectation in her face.

'Yes. I must tell you that I shall be going away soon.'

Emily's face fell. 'Going away? Where?'

'To Australia. I've had the offer of a good job there. I've already made arrangements to have a farewell dinner for all my friends in Rainhill at the Commercial Hotel. It should be a good night.'

Emily's voice came as a kind of croak. As if suddenly her throat had gone very dry. 'But... what? What about us?'

'Yes that does raise a problem. You see I couldn't possibly ask you to accompany me all the way to Australia.' He looked down at her with concern on his face. Then it took on a questioning look and one eyebrow lifted. 'Unless it was as my wife?'

'What did you say?'

'Emily. I'm asking you to be my wife. I can't get down on one knee as although this is a nice new concrete floor I might get my trousers dirty.' He slipped his hand round her waist.

Emily quickly backed away. 'Keep your hands to yourself, Albert Williams!

'Well then while you are thinking about it, why don't we dance?' And he decorously took her right hand in his, slipped his other hand round her waist again and swung her round in a waltz. But what young Emily Mather didn't realise as they swirled round the empty kitchen to the pleasant singing voice of her beau was that the new floor beneath her covered the dead bodies of four people. All of them murdered by Albert Williams!

Frederick Deeming, drawn from a photograph and a description from a fellow passenger.

Of course, his name was not Albert Williams, it was Frederick Bailey Deeming, but he was a man of many aliases and eventually was hunted by the police of three countries. At the time he was as famous – or infamous – as Jack the Ripper; in fact some people still think that he was Jack the Ripper, but this is very unlikely. There is little evidence that he was in London at the time of the crimes, but he was certainly a major international serial killer and is thought to have murdered at least six people, if not more, for moving around the world as he did, he probably escaped detection by many police forces. But in his chequered career he came to Hull and Beverley and the woman he married there was lucky that she too did not end up under a layer of concrete.

Frederick Deeming was born in Birkenhead, just across the Mersey from Liverpool and on the Wirral peninsula, in the year 1852. It is said that he was the seventh child (large families were the norm in those days), and that his father was eventually confined in an insane asylum. He claimed that he had been abused by his father, but was very much attached to his mother and later said that visions of his mother instructed him to kill women. But he was such a practiced liar that little he said could be taken as true.

Not much is known about his early life. He certainly went to Australia in his early twenties, but then he turned up in the Kimberley diamond mines in Cape Province, South Africa in 1877, hoping to make his fortune. It seems that he didn't, and he returned to England. In 1881 he married a Welsh woman from Pembroke called Marie James, with whom he was to have four children. But the next year he was off to Australia again, working his passage as a steward on a liner and leaving his wife behind until such time as he could make enough money to send for her. He worked in Sydney as a plumber and gas fitter and though there was plenty of work going in the young city, he didn't make money quickly enough for him and he began to steal gas fittings. He sent for his wife only a few days before he was arrested and sentenced to prison. But, possibly because this was a first offence in Sydney, he got out of jail just as his wife and family landed in Australia.

There then followed a period of relative stability, until he opened a shop. But although Deeming undoubtedly had 'the gift of the gab' and could charm people easily, he was not reliable enough to succeed as a shopkeeper, and the business went bust. During the bankruptcy proceedings he was arrested for fraud, but while out on bail fled with his family to Port Adelaide. While there he took a short sea voyage and managed to con two brothers out of £60, a considerable sum in those days, and with that he and his family embarked for South Africa.

There he continued his life of crime and managed to con several business men out of substantial sums of money with stories of bogus gold mines. But again it got too hot for him and he and his family fled to Cape Town and then to England. He appeared in Hull in October 1889. He had left his family in Birkenhead, staying with his brother. He presented himself in Hull as an Australian millionaire and the relative of a prominent English MP. He moved in the high society of Hull and Beverley, spent lavishly and entertained rich and influential people. At the time he called himself Lawson.

He met a young lady in Beverley. She was daughter of the lady with whom he had lodgings and was called Nellie Matheson. He courted her and in March 1890, the couple were married in St Mary's church, Beverley. But it seems that local people were becoming suspicious of the flamboyant and fast-talking man from the Antipodes and Deeming decided to cut his losses and run. But he would have one last coup. He exerted all his charm as well as forged references and managed to obtain £285 worth of jewellery from Reynoldsons of Whitefriargate, using a cheque, which subsequently bounced, to pay for it.

He had just arrived at the Royal Station Hotel in Hull with Nellie for their honeymoon, when he told her that he had to go away for a short period on business and left rapidly. He had already booked his passage on the SS *Coleridge*, which was due to sail the following day from Southampton to South America and he caught the next train south from Hull.

St Mary's church in Beverley where Deeming married Nellie Matheson.

But this time Deeming's seemingly incredible luck had run out. He was still in touch with his wife Marie, who must have been aware of at least some of his criminal activities and to a certain extent, went along with them. But when he phoned Marie in Birkenhead and told her that he had married Nellie and that if the police arrived looking for him she was to tell them that she was not married to him, it was the last straw. She went post haste to Beverley to see Nellie, who by this time had reluctantly gone back home. And the two women went to the police.

The Hull police were already on Deeming's trail, for his dud cheque had quickly been discovered, but here was a further charge which could be levelled against him, that of bigamy. The police found out that Deeming had boarded the ship for South America. It was discovered where the next port of call would be – it turned out to be Montevideo – and cables were sent to that city asking that Deeming be arrested and held in connection with the stealing of jewellery.

When the ship entered the port a police launch went out to the ship and Deeming was taken into custody, much to the surprise of the passengers. They had been much impressed by the loquacious and friendly gentleman who had been elected as chairman of the concert in aid of the Seamen's Mission and who had generously headed the subscription list. It took several months to get Deeming back to this country, but finally in October 1890 he stood in the dock at Hull and was sentenced to nine months imprisonment.

When he was released from the Hedon Road jail in July 1891 he went to Rainhill, where he rented the villa in Lawton Road. He said that he wanted it for six months and gave out that it was for the mythical Col. Brooks. But the colonel had a strange request: he disliked the uneven tile floors in the kitchen and the scullery and wanted them re-laid in concrete, and this was

Royal Station Hotel in the early 1900s, where Nellie and Deeming were supposed to have their honeymoon. (courtesy of Memory Lane)

included in the rental agreement. Deeming then set about digging large holes in the floors of the two rooms.

As usual for Deeming he began an attachment with a young lady, an Emily Mather. And when she questioned him about having been seen in various tea establishments with another woman – it was a small town and gossip got round very quickly – he explained that it was his sister. Her husband, he said, would be going to California shortly and his sister would be staying at the villa briefly, before embarking on a ship with her children for America.

In August he did the dreadful deed. He murdered Marie and her four children and buried their bodies under the kitchen and scullery floors, himself mixing and laying the cement over them. Then he collected his wife's and children's clothes, packed them in trunks and sent them on to Plymouth railway station 'to be called for'. Then this callous brute went to his farewell dinner at the Commercial Hotel, entertaining his guests with songs from his extensive repertoire.

On 22 September he married Emily Mather and they honeymooned at New Brighton and on the South Coast and then embarked for Australia on the SS *Kaiser Wilhelm II*. On the journey Emily's letters home, which had begun full of happiness and hope, changed to more subdued epistles as Deeming began his usual practice of flirting with all the pretty women on board and keeping very late hours drinking in the bar. In addition he told Emily that he was going to change their name and when they arrived in Melbourne on 15 December they were Mr and Mrs Droven.

A drawing of Whitefriargate in 1892 where the Reynoldsons were conned out of jewellery by Deeming. (courtesy of Hull Library)

They took a small house in Andrew Street, Windsor, a suburb of Melbourne, and within a few days bags of cement arrived at the house. Early in January Deeming moved into a hotel on his own, and arranged to sell the effects of the house, and a 'To Let' sign went up outside. Within a fortnight Deeming used eight different aliases and stayed at six different hotels – and left, of course, without paying his bill at each one. He also called at a matrimonial agency saying that he was seeking a wife. He wrote to several women and briefly became engaged to one, but none of them suited him.

He then embarked on a short cruise to Sydney on the coastal steamer *Adelaide* using yet another alias – Baron Swanston. Here he met a pretty eighteen-year-old heiress, Kate Rounsfell. He exerted all his charm on the young girl and presented her with some jewellery which he said he had bought for his previous fiancé who had ditched him. In reality, he had conned Kilpatrick & Co., a Melbourne firm, out of the jewellery. But his quixotic gesture endeared him to the young lady and it also impressed her parents, for when she disembarked at Sydney he went with her and asked them formally for permission to marry her.

They agreed and yet another young woman took the first steps towards an early grave. But she was over the moon about this magnetic man who seemed to have so much power and influence over women. Her parents agreed to an early engagement and Deeming gave her a magnificent ring, which he had stolen from yet another jeweller. He then said that he had been offered a job in Western Australia as a mining engineer and he would go there and when he had bought a house for them he would send for her and they would be married. The house he chose would of course be in the most isolated part of this large, and at that time very sparsely populated, land. And just to make sure that she did not lose interest he kept up

Hull Prison in the early 1900s. Deeming spent nine months there in 1890/1. (courtesy of Memory Lane)

a shoal of telegrams and love letters to her. Finally he sent her £20 for her journey and she set out to join him.

Eight weeks after the last tenant had left the house in Andrew Street, Windsor, the agent paid a visit. He couldn't understand why tenants seemed loath to occupy the place, but when he got there he understood. There was an extremely unpleasant and overpowering smell about the house. And when he entered he noticed that the smell seemed to be coming from one of the downstairs rooms. A new concrete hearth stone had been laid, but whoever had laid it had not reckoned with the heat of an Australian summer. It was now badly cracked and the smell was plainly coming from there. He pulled aside lumps of concrete and found himself looking at the corpse of a young woman.

The police were called and soon two detectives were on the scene, DS Considine and Detective Cawsey. Considine asked the agent about the last tenant.

'He said his name was Droven and he took the place with his wife. They didn't have any references since they had just arrived from England. This would be about 16 December. He paid three weeks rent in advance.'

Deeming's description was circulated in Melbourne and in the meantime the two detectives returned to the house. They searched it from top to bottom looking for clues to the previous occupiers and their whereabouts. But there was very little left behind. There were no letters or papers or anything to identify the couple. All that remained was a pile of ash in one of the grates in a downstairs room. But Cawsey was a meticulous searcher and he carefully raked through the pile and came across the charred remains of a medicine bottle. It had a burnt label on it and they could just make out the first three letters of the word 'poison' on it. Then Cawsey found something else.

'Look at this,' he said as he held up a small fragment of a white card. Most of it was burnt, but they could see that it was an invitation card. 'Mr Albert Williams requests the pleasure of the company of –', he read out. 'And then there's more: "dinner at the Commercial Hotel, Rainhill."'

Considine nodded his head. 'I'll bet that Albert Williams or Droven is an alias. But where on earth is Rainhill?' They pored over maps and gazetteers for several hours until they discovered that there was a Rainhill near Liverpool in England. Cables passed between Melbourne and Scotland Yard asking for information about an Albert Williams and the Australian police were told that Williams was really Frederick Bailey Deeming. Subsequently the Liverpool police went to the villa in Rainhill and there, because of what had been found in Windsor, dug up the newly laid concrete floor and discovered the bodies of Marie Deeming and her four children.

In Melbourne the circulation of Deeming's description among hotel and boarding houses, shops and ports was bringing results. The police discovered he had been using a bewildering series of aliases, and they had many reports of jewellers having been conned out of valuable pieces. But Considine was in a quandary: he didn't think that Deeming had left the country, because there were no reports of a man of his description boarding a ship, but he had no idea where he was. He decided on a desperate gamble: he would ask newspapers to print a picture of Deeming with a wanted notice. It was a very unusual practice at the time, but it brought immediate results.

Kate Rounsfell picked up a paper one morning on her journey to Western Australia and in it saw a picture of her fiancé, wanted for murder! She went back to Melbourne immediately and contacted the police. They telegraphed the Perth police and Deeming was picked up in the small mining town of Southern Cross. He was brought back to Melbourne by train, but the publicity generated by the newspaper reports resulted in crowds besieging the train at every stop wanting to lynch the prisoner.

At his trial in Melbourne for the murder of Emily Mather, before Mr Justice Hodges, his defence was insanity. He complained of hallucinations and mental disturbances and claimed that the spirit of his dead mother was constantly urging him to kill women. But the jury would have none of it and found him guilty of murder and added a rider that they did not think he was insane. At this he began a tirade saying that the jury had been influenced by the press.

'When this extraordinary scene was enacted in court,' reported the *London Times*, 'daylight faded into darkness, gas and candles were lit and the whole scene was weird in the extreme.'

But the sentence of death was passed, his appeal was dismissed and on 23 May 1892 Deeming was hanged under the name of Williams. It is reported that the hangman wore a false white beard and his assistant a false black one to avoid identification, as there were a large number of ticket holders to watch the event.

2

'My Girl must not be Involved'

This case has been described as one of the most remarkable in the history of British criminology. It began quietly enough on a Wednesday in late September in the year 1923. Henry Williams was out picking blackberries in an area known as Long Valley, near Aldershot. As he approached a small copse on the fringe of the Long Valley, he saw a pair of boots sticking up from the surrounding undergrowth. They were under some gorse bushes on a patch of marshy ground. He came closer and saw that there appeared to be a body attached to the boots. It was clothed in an Army uniform. But it had obviously been there for a long time, for the tunic crumbled away to dust when he touched it and he could see the white of bones beneath it. He rushed away to find a policeman and report his find.

Police officers were soon on the scene and Superintendent Davies, chief of the Aldershot CID, was informed. When he viewed the body near the copse he saw that the word 'Leicester' appeared on the shoulder tags of the tunic and on the arm was a badge showing a drum. This rang a bell. A soldier had gone missing in the May of that year from the 1st Battalion of the Leicester Regiment, which occupied the Badajos Barracks, near the Royal Garrison church in Aldershot. And he had been posted as a deserter. He was Drummer James Frederick Ellis, whose home was in Alpha Avenue, Nornabell Street, Hull.

But identification was still uncertain as the body was almost completely skeletonised. But Sergeant Drummer Ormes, who was in charge of the band section, came forward to say that Ellis, who had been in the band, had some teeth missing in the front. Two years before, Ellis, who had been a bugler, had come to Sgt Ormes and complained that he could no longer blow his bugle because he had lost some of his front teeth. He had then been given the job of a side drummer. Subsequently Ellis had obtained some false teeth when he was stationed in Ireland.

The false teeth were not found with the body, but they turned up later in the strangest way. In the June after Ellis had disappeared, two boy scouts, Jack Court and his friend Rickwood, were in the Long Valley when Rickwood found a bottom dental plate with three teeth on it. It was found some distance away from where the body was later discovered, but the boys didn't see the body. Court found another plate, the upper one this time, not far away. He tied them both to his scout pole and took them home. But his mother wouldn't have them in the house and told him to bury them in the garden, which he did. Several months later when the discovery of the body was reported in the newspapers, Jack Court's father, who was a departmental manager of a local printing firm, remembered the buried dental plates. He dug them up, cleaned them and took them to the police and they fitted the skull perfectly.

Photocopy of a portion of the *Daily Mail* for 29 September 1923. (courtesy of *Hull Daily Mail*)

The body had been trussed up thoroughly with drum cord. The hands had been roped behind the back and the ankles tied together. In the jaws of the skull a rolled up piece of cloth was found and another piece had been tied tightly round the lower part of the face. In addition an Army greatcoat had been wrapped around the head and closely secured with a webbing belt.

At first it was thought that the death was the result of some bizarre sexual practice Ellis had indulged in which had gone horribly wrong. Sir Bernard Spilsbury, called in by the Hampshire police because of the puzzling nature of the case, disagreed. Sir Bernard Spilsbury was the most famous pathologist of his day and had been involved in every important murder enquiry from the Crippen case in 1910 to the Antiquis murder trial in 1947. And the police, judges, counsel and even juries believed implicitly that Spilsbury was always right. Spilsbury wrote in his report that Ellis could not have trussed himself up. 'The ligature round the mouth must have been tight and with the rolled up cloth he would be securely gagged. The belt also must have been tight. This could not have been done by the deceased. He would have been unable to call out or talk.' The cause of death, he asserted, was suffocation, probably within ten minutes of Ellis being tied up.

Some scraps of paper had been found in the pocket of the tunic. They had almost crumbled away to dust, but a few names could be made out on the pieces which were left. Sgt Ormes identified the names as members of the drum section. Also associated with them were figures representing sums of money. Possibly then, Ellis had been a money lender. Was it likely that a man who was in his debt and couldn't pay might have murdered him? The method of murder, though, pointed to a certain anger on the part of the murderer. It was a cruel way to kill anybody, to just tie them up and leave them to suffocate. And then there was the question, would Ellis have calmly submitted to being tied up, unless it was someone he knew and trusted?

It was obvious that it had to be a friend of his or at least someone he knew pretty well and the police began investigating the soldiers that Ellis had come into contact with. In fact, a large number of soldiers were taken to the police office in Aldershot and individually questioned, even some from outside Ellis's own unit. A couple of soldiers from a cavalry regiment were questioned about a man they saw at about the time the Ellis disappeared carrying a sack over his shoulder in the vicinity of where the body was afterwards discovered.

But it was a letter from Ellis's girlfriend, Miss Ivy Wainfer, who lived at Walter's Terrace, Waller Street, Hull, that pointed the finger at a possible suspect. She and Ellis had been going together for about a year and he used to write to her two or three times a week when he was away. She had last seen him when he was home for four days at Easter and he had seemed in good spirits. When he didn't write anymore she was very upset, but believed as most other people did that he had deserted. But when she heard that his body had been discovered and there was the

Waller Street in the 1920s. Ellis' girlfriend Ivy Wainfer lived here. (courtesy of Hull Library)

likelihood that he had been murdered, she remembered something that Ellis had written about in his last letters. He said that he had fallen out with a soldier, who had been his best friend, over a girl. Ivy Wainfer then wrote to the police telling them what Ellis had written.

The man was twenty-year-old L/Cpl Albert Edward Dearnley and he lived just across the street from Ellis in Alpha Avenue, Nornabell Street. They had been friends from an early age and had attended Buckingham Street School together. After they left school they both had periods of unemployment and they decided to join the Army together.

There was a training battalion of the 1st Leicester Regiment stationed at Hedon and both of them enlisted in the band section, Ellis as a bugler and Dearnley as a drummer boy. Their friendship seemed to have its ups and down, but they apparently remained friends. Dearnley had been questioned when Ellis first disappeared in May, but he said then that Ellis had told him he was fed up with the Army and was going to desert. He had been seen with Ellis on the day he disappeared, they had gone out for a walk together, but he said that they split up and he returned alone. When Ellis did not return, Dearnley assumed that he had made good his intention of absconding.

The police questioned Dearnley again when they received the letter from Ivy Wainfer, pointing out that Ellis had not deserted as he had said and since he was the last person to see him alive he had some explaining to do. Dearnley changed his story. He now said that originally he and Ellis had talked about deserting, but that Ellis had wanted to go first to Hull to get some money and take a passage to America. But then Dearnley became involved with a woman. She was the sister-in-law of Sgt Ormes and her name was Hilda Storey. She was a dressmaker in Bishop Auckland and Dearnley had first seen her photograph in Sgt Ormes's quarters when he was the sergeant's batman. But for some reason he couldn't explain Ellis had become jealous of his friendship with Hilda Storey and had taken to being rude to her. Once at a dance he had called her an old cow.

On the day that Ellis disappeared the two had been drinking and then had gone for a walk outside the barracks in Long Valley. They had been messing about playing Cowboys and Indians and Ellis had boasted that if Dearnley tied him up he could get free and be back at the camp before Dearnley got there. So the lance corporal had tied him up and had gone back to camp, fully expecting that Ellis would be there waiting for him. And when he didn't turn up he assumed that Ellis had indeed deserted.

But the police didn't believe him, since they had Sir Bernard Spilsbury's evidence that Ellis was bound too tightly to allow him to escape. And he gave this evidence at the police court hearing and at the trial, held at the Winchester Assizes in November 1923, before Mr Justice Avory. At his trial Dearnley pleaded that he had no intention of killing Ellis, although he had to admit it was a stupid thing to do to tie him up as he did. But the jury didn't believe him and found him guilty of murder. The judge pronounced the death sentence on 27 November 1923.

There was consternation in Hull. Although the murdered man had also been a native of the city, it was felt that because of Dearnley's age and because there was a lingering doubt in many people's minds that perhaps he hadn't really meant to do it, the death sentence was too severe. An appeal against the sentence was lodged by Dearnley's lawyers, but the trial judge said that he fully agreed with the jury's verdict and the prisoner's demeanour had been 'callous throughout the trial'. The appeal was dismissed. The fight for a reprieve was taken up by his vicar, the Revd E.A. Berry of Drypool, who wrote to the Home Office, as did many other people in East Hull. A petition was raised with a great many signatures and this was handed in to the Home Office in London.

But it was announced on Saturday 5 January 1924 that the Revd Berry had received a message from the home secretary saying that he 'had failed to find any grounds which would justify him advising His Majesty to interfere with the due course of the law.' The execution would take place on the following Tuesday, 8 January, at 9.00 a.m.

The funeral of James Ellis showing the coffin above, and below is the tragic figure of Dearnley's father supported by two friends. Inset is a portrait of Ellis. Taken from the *Daily Mail* for 8 October 1923.

Dearnley's father and his step-mother made the long journey by train from Hull to the jail at Winchester and were allowed to see their son for the last time. The interview was at 8.30 in the morning and they were allowed just fifteen minutes with him. Mrs Dearnley said afterwards that her stepson was seated 10ft away from them, between two warders who would be with him every minute of the day or night until his execution, just to make sure he didn't cheat the hangman by committing suicide. His parents were allowed no contact with their son, except for a greeting and a parting hug when they left. His father said that his son was quiet and brave and did not break down. He asked him if anyone else was involved, but he would not answer. But then he said, 'my girl must not be involved.'

When his parents had finally made their sad journey back to Hull, they called in at their son's grandparents' house to break the news to them. But they were amazed when they got there. The grandparents told them that it had just been announced that the death sentence had been postponed! And very soon after that came the news that Dearnley had been reprieved. His sentence had been commuted to life imprisonment.

But what caused the sudden turnaround? Never before in British legal history had a halt come at such a late stage, with the execution only hours away. What was the reason for it? According to A.A. Clarke in his very entertaining book *The Groaning Gallows*, this is the explanation:

The firing party at Ellis's funeral with arms reversed preceding the cortege, taken from the *Daily Mail* for 8 September 1923.

Three days before he was due to hang Dearnley sat down to write a last letter to Hilda Storey. He wrote that he wanted her to have his watch as there was nothing else he had to give her to remember him by. But he also decided to tell her a secret which he had been keeping for the whole time since the death of Drummer Ellis, all through the period until the body was discovered, the trial and finally his last imprisonment.

As was the case at the time the letter had to be read by the prison governor and when he saw the contents he interviewed Dearnley in his cell. Dearnley had stated in his letter that when he was Sgt Ormes's batman he had been introduced to homosexuality by the sergeant. During one of these episodes they were surprised by Ellis who threatened to go to the authorities, since at that time homosexual activity was illegal even between consenting adults. Ellis then blackmailed Dearnley into having sex with him. But when Dearnley began to go out with Hilda Storey, Ellis became extremely jealous and threatened to tell the girl what had been going on with him and her brother-in-law, unless he gave her up. It was this which had caused Dearnley to finally snap and kill his friend.

This of course put a different complexion on the case. The prison governor asked the prison doctor to examine Dearnley and he confirmed that the young man had indeed been involved in homosexual activity. The governor immediately contacted the Home Office in London and they instituted a search for Sgt Ormes. He was finally located and asked to attend the Home Office for an interview on 7 January. The day before Dearnley was due to hang.

At the interview it was explained to the sergeant that though homosexual activity was a criminal offence, under the present circumstances he would not be prosecuted if he told the truth. And the sergeant finally admitted that Dearnley's story was true.

This was all very well, but only the home secretary himself, Lord Bridgeman, could sanction the halting of the hanging, and he was at home in Shropshire. He was finally reached by telephone and agreed that had the jury known of the true circumstances behind the death of Ellis, their verdict could well have been different. The hanging was postponed and eventually Dearnley was reprieved.

3

Murder at the Institution

In March 1871 Charles Sleight was thirty-two. From the age of sixteen he had been living with his older brother William, who was the manager of the Deaf and Dumb Institution at Brighton. These were institutions, often run by the churches, which gave classes to young children during the day and adults in the evenings to give them an education they couldn't get at ordinary schools and to teach them sign language.

The term 'deaf and dumb' was popular in the eighteenth and nineteenth century, as was the term 'mutes', which the inmates were called, but the terms today are offensive to deaf and hard of hearing people: most deaf people are not dumb at all, since their vocal chords are not affected, but not being able to hear yourself speak makes it difficult to formulate and produce understandable speech. However, they can communicate by sign language, lip reading and sometimes even by vocalisations.

Charles and his brother William were not deaf and could both speak normally. William, who was an expert in the sign language used at the time, had taught his brother to use it and in time Charles became a teacher at the institution. A deeply religious young man, he was a great reader, though mainly of biblical works and religious commentaries and tracts. From an early age he had been troubled with intense pains in the head, which he told his friends were due to the fact that a school master had once lifted him up by his ears.

The time came for Charles to move on, and he applied for and was accepted as the manager of the Kingston-upon-Hull branch of the Institution for the Deaf of Yorkshire and Lincolnshire, which occupied a building at No. 10 Dock Street. It was later reported that the vacancy occurred because the previous incumbent had been dismissed for misbehaviour with some of his charges.

He first came to Hull in November 1870 and took lodgings in Brough, on the bank of the Humber, and there he met a Miss Jacques. They became friendly and their friendship ripened into an engagement. But Charles moved from there and lived first at St Luke's Street and then at No. 3 St James Place. This time he lodged with John and Maria Hailstone. Both were profoundly deaf, but John was a skilled painter and worked for Mr Tom Stainforth and his father, who ran a painting and decorating business in Clarendon Street. He had been treated very well by the firm who took him on as an apprentice when he was thirteen or fourteen years old. Tom Stainforth went so far as to learn sign language himself so he could better communicate with John.

Early in 1871 Charles Sleight and John and Maria Hailstone moved into the institution building at No. 10 Dock Street. It was a large house and John and Maria had a bedroom on the top floor. John continued to work for Mr Stainforth and Maria became the matron, doing the

Clarendon Street today, where the Stainforths ran their painting and decorating business.

cooking and cleaning, generally looking after the classrooms downstairs on the ground floor and helping out with the children. Both were still quite young, Maria being twenty-two and her husband twenty-seven.

But it seems that Charles was not happy. Perhaps he missed the companionship of his elder brother. He wrote to his sister Jane Sleight, who was living in Harrogate, saying that he was feeling lonely and he wished he hadn't left Brighton. He had nobody to talk to. There was always John and Maria, but possibly he found it difficult to have long discussions with them. He certainly complained that he had to answer the front door himself as the others could not hear the bell. He also wrote that he felt that his mind was going away. He said, 'My head spins as if it were tightly strapped and terrible fancies keep passing through my head.'

On Saturday 18 March he took Miss Jacques and Maria on an excursion trip to New Holland. On the way back he seemed very despondent. He closed his eyes and told Miss Jacques that he felt very sad. On the following Tuesday he turned up at the residence of Mr Thomas Haller, who was the secretary and treasurer of the Deaf Institution and lived in Anlaby Road. Haller, who had been instrumental in having Charles Sleight appointed as manager, had always been very friendly and supportive of the young man, but he was surprised to see him that early in the morning just as he had finished breakfast.

Sleight told him that he had been to the doctor's and that he was very ill. He looked pale, very nervous and agitated. His hands were twitching and he said he felt cold. Haller said that he would go back with him to the home. On the way Sleight seemed anxious about the school and asked him, 'What will happen to the dear children?'

'I'll see to that. Let's get you to bed.'

He was as good as his word: he saw Charles into his bed, which was on the first floor, and then went down to the children on the ground floor. He stayed with them for an hour, although he didn't speak sign language too well himself, then he went to see Maria. He told her to take charge of the children until noon while he went into another room and wrote letters to all their parents telling them to keep the children at home until Thursday morning. Then he sent the children home with their letters. Before he left he asked Maria to make Sleight a little gruel.

He called again the next day. The doctor was there this time and Haller asked him what he thought about his patient. The doctor seemed puzzled and was vague about the cause of Charles's illness, but he said that he had prescribed some medicine which Charles had taken. When Haller saw Sleight however, the young man complained that the medicine was not working and asked Haller to fetch him ½oz of caster oil, which he did.

Charles Sleight was visited on the same day by his niece Emma Smith who lived in Beverley. She thought that he looked ill and he was plainly worried about his finances, saying that he had spent a lot of money on furnishing the home and if he were too ill to carry on, would he lose his money? He also said that he had very queer fancies coming into his head.

Haller came again on Thursday expecting to have to take the class but found Charles already in the school room. He persuaded Sleight not to carry on and dismissed the children until Monday morning. On Sunday morning at a quarter past nine, Haller called again. He found Sleight sitting on a sofa in the room that they all used as a sitting room, twitching and looking very agitated. John and Maria were also there, as was Maria's brother, who was also deaf. Charles had the New Testament on his knee which he was trying to read. He looked up as Thomas came into the room.

'Is there forgiveness for such great sinners?' he asked Haller.

Haller asked him what was troubling him.

'If you'll come and sit by me, I'll tell you.' He looked round at the others, but plainly although they could see that something was going on they couldn't tell what it was. But perhaps Sleight felt that they could read his lips. He leaned towards Haller when he sat by him. 'I've been sorely tempted,' he said.

'Tempted to what?'

'I've been so much shut up alone with Maria that I've been tempted.'

He didn't say what he had been tempted to do, but said that he had taken her in his arms.

Haller frowned and for a while said nothing, while Sleight looked up at him anxiously. 'You must drive all such thoughts from your mind, my boy,' he said eventually. He paused and then continued. 'Come up to my house this afternoon and we will read the Bible together.'

It appeared that Sleight had indeed been having lascivious thoughts about Maria. She told her husband that Sleight had once put his arms around her, pulled her down on to his knee and kissed her. She didn't make a big thing about it to her husband afterwards, merely mentioning it in passing, because both of them had a high regard for the young man. But she did say that she didn't like it. And she said to Sleight that she thought that he ought to get married. In fact Haller had suggested this as well, thinking that it would perhaps settle him down and cure him of these fits of despondency and depression which seemed to attack him.

When he arrived at Haller's house at about three o'clock that Sunday afternoon his attitude was very strange. The housekeeper opened the door for him and he stood looking down on the ground and opening and closing his fists. She recognised him, of course, since he often came to see her employer and she was about to invite him in when he rushed past her and went straight to the sitting-room door, which he opened and went in without knocking. He stood there without taking off his hat or overcoat, looking about him wildly.

Unfortunately Thomas Haller had company. His sister-in-law had arrived unexpectedly and he was in the process of giving her afternoon tea. However, he managed to get the servant to relieve Sleight of his hat and coat and sat him on a chair. Sleight had brought a copy of

Dock Street in 1870, the location of the Deaf Institution. (courtesy of Memory Lane)

Dr Clarke's *Commentary on the New Testament* with him and asked for the Bible, which was given to him. He sat in silence, reading, and took no part in the conversation. After he had had his tea he went back to Dock Street.

The next morning, John Hailstone got up as usual at half past five. He went downstairs to the kitchen to wash and get dressed then went back upstairs to tell his wife he was leaving. She went back to sleep. He closed his bedroom door behind him and passed Sleight's door on the way down and it too was closed. He locked the front door behind him as he had a key and so did Sleight. John caught the six o'clock train to Hessle and began work on Mr Reckitt's house there. At about eleven o'clock that same morning his boss Tom Stainforth arrived. But he had some terrible news for John.

Inspector William Grace was in charge of the police station in Parliament Street that Monday morning. A few minutes after seven Charles Sleight came into the charge room. The inspector was standing behind the counter and asked him what he wanted.

'I wish to see the superintendent.'

'He's not here, but I am the officer in charge at the moment.'

Charles came round the counter and confronted the inspector. 'There has been a young woman murdered in Dock Street.'

'Where?'

'At the Deaf and Dumb School, 10 Dock Street.'

'How was it done? And who did it?'

Sleight held out his left hand. The middle finger was bandaged with some rag, but there was blood on it.

'Did you do it?'

'Yes I did.'

Anlaby Road in 1870, the residence of Thomas Haller. (courtesy of Hull Library)

The inspector pointed to a chair near a desk and told him to sit down and he did so. Then Grace sat behind the desk and prepared to take notes. But suddenly the young man reached forward to grab some papers on the desk and attempted to tear them up. The inspector managed to get them out of his hands, but Sleight dropped the papers and then grabbed a thick wooden ruler on the desk. The inspector wrestled with Sleight trying to get the ruler away from him and shouted for assistance. Then Sleight dropped the ruler, got up, throwing off the inspector, and rushed for the fireplace, where he picked up a poker. But by now a police constable had come from the cell area and the two policemen were able to get the poker from Sleight's grip. He was still struggling and shouting, but more policemen arrived and Sleight was bundled into a cell. They were able to go through his pockets and found some keys. Sleight was then locked up in the cell and the inspector wrote on the charge sheet, for they had to give a reason for locking anyone up in a cell, 'being in an insane state at the police station'.

The inspector took the keys and went to Dock Street. He discovered a key which opened the front door. In the upstairs bedroom he found the body of Maria Hailstone with her throat cut. She lay on the floor with bedclothes around her, wearing only a chemise and a nightdress and, curiously, one stocking. Plainly she had been putting her stockings on when Sleight burst in and in modesty had got back into bed before she was attacked. A razor lay on the floor beside the bed. A search of Sleight's room revealed a bloodstained nightshirt, several razors – it turned out that John Hailstone didn't use a razor – and a sharpening stone with fresh oil upon it.

Charles Sleight went to trial at the York Assizes on 31 July 1871, before Mr Justice Mellor. The prosecution was led by Mr T.B. Thomson and Sleight was defended by Mr Waddy. The defence was obviously one of insanity. His brother William went into the witness box to detail Charles's early history and his tearful account affected many people in court. Jane Sleight reported that an elder brother had committed suicide in Belfast and a coroner's certificate was produced showing that John

SPECIAL EDITION.

HULL TIMES OFFICE, Monday, 6 p.m.

ANOTHER

MURDER IN HULL.

A DEAF AND DUMB WOMAN
MURDERED BY A TEACHER.

Photocopy of a portion of the Hull and
North Lincolnshire Times for 27 March 1871.
(courtesy of *Hull Daily Mail*)

Sleight had cut his throat while in a state of insanity in 1852. An aunt who was eighty-five went into the witness box to tell of another aunt who tried to commit suicide several times and was confined in the asylum in Lincoln and died there. She also told of a cousin who should have gone into an asylum, but whose husband kept her under the care of a keeper; the woman escaped and drowned herself in a millpond. Thomas Garland, who was a cousin of Charles Sleight, said he had a brother who had been confined in the Bedlam Asylum in 1850. Returning home after it was said he was cured he tried to strangle his brother and was returned to the asylum where he now remained.

After this catalogue it seemed that the jury had had enough. The foreman rose to address the bench and said that the jury had made up their minds what verdict they would return. The judge warned the jury that they must be convinced on the evidence before them that the prisoner at the time he committed the dreadful crime was in such a state of mind that he did not know the nature and the character of the act that he was committing, that he did not know it was a wrongful and a wicked act or that it was contrary to law. And only then could they acquit him.

The jury accepted this and then acquitted him on the grounds of insanity, and Charles Sleight was subsequently committed to an asylum.

4

Lucky Murderer

It was half past two on a cold Wednesday afternoon, the first of March 1939, when the ambulance was called to the fire station in Hull. A man had been seen clinging to one of the piles at the entrance to the Victoria Dock, where it met the River Hull, near the rear of Rank's Flour Mill. The firemen using their ladders managed to get the man out of the freezing water and he was taken by ambulance to the Hull Royal Infirmary.

He was a short man with dark hair turning grey and was wearing a blue suit with a white muffler round his throat and he was in a bad way. He had previously told his sister that he had taken 600 aspirin tablets before jumping off the bridge over the lock. At the infirmary the nurses got his soaking clothes off him and put him to bed with hot water bottles. They noticed that he had tattoos on the backs of both forearms and hands. The tattoo on the right forearm was W. Burkitt, and this was repeated as a tattoo on his right hand. Slowly the man began to recover. But as this was a suicide attempt and since suicide was a felony in those days the police were called.

They were pleased to see him since they had been looking for him and on the Saturday at 8.20 a.m. Inspector Barker, accompanied by DS Kilvington, entered the long men's ward at the infirmary and approached the bed, which had curtains pulled around it. They passed the curious stares of the other bed occupants, drew the curtains back and stepped inside.

The inspector spoke. 'We are police officers and –.'

'I know who you are,' snapped Burkitt, who was standing by the side of the bed. 'I know what you are going to say. I don't want to know. I'm not going to listen!' And he turned his back on the two policemen and stood looking down on the floor. For a moment the inspector was nonplussed, but he knew what he had to do. And to make sure that the man heard him he went round and faced Burkitt, who would not look at him. Nevertheless Inspector Barker recited the caution to him and then he said:

At about 12.30 p.m. on Wednesday 1 March I went to No. 5, Pleasant Place, Neptune Street, Hull. There in an upstairs bedroom I saw the dead body of Emma Brookes, lying on a bed. I understand you have been living with this woman. Later the same day I was present at a post-mortem examination when it was ascertained that death had been caused by her being throttled. I am going to take you into custody and you will be charged with the wilful murder of Emma Brookes at that address on or about 27 February 1939.

'When you're ready, I am,' Burkitt replied.

They took him down to the central police station, where he was again cautioned and charged with the murder. He made no reply. The inspector shook his head. He knew that William Burkitt was a trawler man and had been a fireman on the trawler *William Bell*, owned by the Mills Steamship Co. and had only landed in Hull the previous Sunday. This was probably just another case of a fisherman away at sea a lot whose wife or co-habitee had strayed a bit and when he came home he had gone a little too far this time and killed her. There were many stories just like this one. But the inspector could not have been more wrong.

The story of William Burkitt has gone down as one of the most incredible in the annals of crime. All the standard works of crime and criminology carry this unique case. And I make no apology for presenting it here, because it is a uniquely Hull story.

In August 1915 the First World War had been going for a year and there was stalemate on the battlefields of Flanders. Nevertheless the Hull newspapers were full of the casualties that the city had suffered. Whole pages were devoted to the men and woman who had lost their lives or gone missing in the fighting or were lost at sea by enemy action. The East Coast had been mined by the Germans and trawler men from both sides of the Humber volunteered to do the very dangerous job of sweeping the mines.

One of these was twenty-eighty-year-old William Burkitt, but after a spell with the minesweeping fleet, he began fishing out of Scarborough. But he came home to Hull for

Victoria Dock in 1939, from which Burkitt was pulled after his failed suicide attempt. (courtesy of Memory Lane)

periods and on 21 August 1915 he arrived back in Hull, going straight to No. 4 Derwent Avenue, Westbourne Street. Westbourne Street does not exist today. It used to lie midway between Eastbourne Street and Hawthorne Avenue and was one of the many streets which were parallel to each other and ran north off the Hessle Road and roughly opposite the St Andrews Dock. This was the first dock built in Hull, entirely for fishing vessels. It was constructed in 1883. Derwent Avenue was one of the small terraces which ran at right angles off the main street and was opposite the Westbourne Street School nearest to the Hessle Road.

There lived Mary Jane Tyler, who was thirty-four and living apart from her husband Arthur, who was a private in the East Yorkshire Regiment. She had done so for about the past twelve years and most of that time she had been living with George Harding, who was a fisherman. But as was the case with some common-law wives of fishermen, when he was at sea she would have other fishermen to live with her. The money that they brought in was useful, since she had two children, Flora and George, and in those days family allowances did not exist.

Another and more recent view of Victoria Dock showing the lock gates. (courtesy of Memory Lane)

One of these temporary lodgers was William Burkitt. He became obsessed with Mary Tyler, whom he called Polly. He had known her for a couple of years since she had lived next door to his mother, who at that time lived in Scarborough Street, which leads south off Hessle Road. Burkitt knew that she had other men living with her and was extremely jealous. But there seemed to be little that he could do about it. On the other hand, Polly was quite emotional herself and their relationship was very quarrelsome.

When Burkitt arrived on Saturday 21 August 1915 things seemed to be going well for them, but by the following Thursday quarrels had broken out. Polly found a photograph in his pocket of Burkitt with his arm round a girl.

'What's this?' she shouted.

'It's only a picture of some girl I know in Scarborough.'

'Well why have you got your arms around her?'

'It's only one of those pictures they take of you on the prom. The photographer told me to put my arm around her as it made a better picture.'

'I don't believe you. You *******', she swore at him. She tore the snap up and flung the pieces in his face. 'You're a *******', she started to swear at him again. Then she struck him in the face. 'Go back to your girl in Scarborough! I don't want you!'

'No, but you'll take my money won't you? I'm going to stay.'

She swore at him again.

'If you call me that again I'll blind you. I'll do for you if you're not careful. And as for that long length of ********, I'll do for him when he comes home.'

It seems that they might even have come to blows, but they seemed to have patched things up later and went out drinking together. But by the end of the evening they were quarrelling again. Polly went to her next-door neighbour, Mrs Elizabeth Houghton, and said that she was afraid to stay in the house with Billy and could she stay the night? Mrs Houghton agreed. The next day Polly went back home and Mrs Houghton heard no more quarrelling from next door. Eliza, Mrs Houghton's daughter, saw them out together that Saturday afternoon and they seemed to be in good spirits, although she thought that Burkitt was drunk. Later they were on their own as Flora and George had gone to the pictures.

But at a quarter to nine that night Burkitt's mother, who lived at No. 1 Worcester terrace, Gillette Street, the next street, but one, from Scarborough Street, arrived home to find her son in her house in distressed condition. 'Mother', he said, 'I've done it!'

'What have you done now?'

'I've done Polly in! She won't tantalise anyone else! Come with me and I'll show you.' They went round to the house in Devonshire Avenue and Burkitt gave his mother the key. She opened the door, but the place was in darkness, so Burkitt went ahead and lit the gas.

'Where is she?'

Burkitt pointed to the far corner of the room. 'She won't tantalise anyone else,' he repeated.

They went back to Gillette Street after Burkitt had locked up the house again. His brother Harold was there this time and Burkitt told his brother what he had done. He handed him a knife which was covered in blood and also bent with the force of the blow or blows he must have inflicted and he showed him his hands which were also bloodstained. He took off his belt and gave it to his brother, together with his lucky halfpenny. 'Keep these,' he said, 'as a remembrance of me.' Then he ran off up Gillette Street saying that he was going to kill himself. But he met Polly's two children on their way home from the cinema. He grabbed George by the arm and handed him the front door key. 'Go and fetch a policeman. Tell him your mother is dead!' Then he raced away. The children quickly found PC Marshall and he went with them to Devonshire Avenue. He made them wait outside while he went in and

Drawing of William Burkitt from the *Hull Times* for 11 September 1915. (courtesy of *Hull Daily Mail*)

investigated. He found the body of Mary Tyler fully clothed lying in a corner on the room. It was later determined that she had been stabbed four times and the one in the neck had caused her death.

PC Marshall, who knew Burkitt, went searching for him the next morning and found him curled up inside a large drainpipe on some waste ground, near his mother's home in Gillette Street. He was asleep. The officer arrested him and on the way to Gordon Street Police Station Burkitt told him that Polly had thrown her wedding ring at him. He asked, 'did you find the ring?' Marshall said that he had not, but that he would look for it, and he found it later in the living room.

William Burkitt was brought to trial at York Assizes in November, before Mr Justice Atkin, and charged with murder. He was defended by Mr Rowan Hamilton, who had been appointed by the court since Burkitt had no money to pay counsel. The prosecution was in the hands of Mr H.S. Cautley MP and Mr Stranger and they had no difficulty establishing a convincing case against Burkitt. Indeed the judge informed the jury before the trial started that he thought they would have no difficulty in returning a verdict of guilty of murder.

Mr Hamilton had an almost impossible task. But he did the best he could, pointing out that Burkitt had received great provocation from Mary Tyler, who continually nagged him and had stuck him and pointed out that the act of killing her must have been committed in a frenzy. But the judge in his summing up said that mere nagging was no justification for violence and if possession of a nagging wife were sufficient to reduce the charge to manslaughter it would be a dangerous thing. But the all male jury ignored him. Perhaps they felt sympathy for the prisoner or perhaps the emotional evidence of Mrs Burkitt as she tearfully defended her son swayed the jury. At all events, they brought in a verdict of guilty of manslaughter and the judge sentenced Burkitt to twelve years penal servitude.

He actually served nine years (having a reduced sentence because of good behaviour) and was released in 1924. He went back to live with his mother in Gillette Street and continued to work as a fisherman. The third street to the east of Gillett Street was Subway Street. A typical fisherman's area; there were fish-curing plants near the end of the street and many small terraces leading off it. One of these was Leslie Avenue and there lived Mrs Ellen Spencer. Her marital state was much the same as Mary Tyler's had been. She was separated from her husband and living off and on with Harry Sargeson, who was a cook on a trawler, and therefore away at sea a good deal. And when Harry Sargeson was away William Burkitt paid court to Mrs Spencer.

Less than a year after Burkitt had been released from prison Mrs Spencer's daughter Mrs Matilda Walkington paid a visit to her mother's house. Although it was midday she saw that the blinds were drawn. Going round the back she found that the back door had been secured with string. She called a neighbour for help and he cut the string and opened the door. Inside there was a strong smell of gas and in the living room was the body of her mother. She had been stabbed in the neck and was dead.

The neighbour went for the police. PC Arthur Douthwaite also smelt the gas as he searched the house. In the upstairs front bedroom he found Burkitt lying unconscious on the bed. The officer turned off the gas and opened all the windows then attempted to revive Burkitt. He managed to get the dazed man conscious enough to walk him about and during that time, according to the PC, Burkitt confessed to the murder. He said he had stabbed Mrs Spencer because he was jealous of another man. He even told the officer where he could find the murder weapon and PC Douthwaite duly found a knife in a kitchen drawer. Although it didn't appear to have any blood on it, forensic examination later did turn up traces of blood on it and a coat and some trousers which Burkitt admitted were his were found to be soaked in blood.

When the ambulance had taken Burkitt to the infirmary he was interviewed again by the police and then made a written confession to the murder. But when he went to trial again at York Assizes the defence ridiculed the confession claiming that it was worthless, being obtained from a man obviously under the effects of coal-gas poisoning.

Burkitt himself went into the witness box to claim that he couldn't remember making any statement to the police. But he could remember, he said, the circumstances of the evening. He had drunk seven pints of beer in a pub and then went to Mrs Spencer's house. He was dozing on a couch when he felt her hand in his pocket. He jumped up and knocked the woman over. He didn't realise what he had in his hand until he saw the blood and realised what must have happened. He put it down to the drink.

This was a major part of the defence case (that he was so insensible by drink that he didn't know what he was doing). He strenuously denied being jealous of the other man and the defence claimed that there was no evidence that he was. He was lucky in that the judge, Sir Hugh Fraser, considered that there was element of doubt. 'If the scales of justice are balanced evenly for and against the prisoner,' he said, 'then it is the duty of the judge to put into the balance a few grains of mercy', because at that time a conviction for murder automatically included a date with the hangman.

St Andrew's Dock. (courtesy of Memory Lane)

The jury are never told of the previous convictions of an accused person before they bring in their verdict, except under certain very rare circumstances, and thus the jury knew nothing about his previous escape from the gallows. They agreed with the judge and came down on the side of mercy and brought in a verdict of guilty only to manslaughter. This time he was awarded ten years in prison.

Burkitt served his full ten years and was released in 1935. He returned as always to the fishing community he knew best, around the Hessle Road, and again went to sea as a trawler man. And then, as if the fates were looking down and preparing a situation for his destruction, William Burkitt met another woman. She was just like all the others. Mrs Emma Brookes was separated from her husband, who was a fisherman and who had been fishing out of Grimsby, but just before the tragedy had arrived back in Hull. He had been paying his wife 25 shillings a week, subsequently reduced to 17 shillings a week under a court separation order, but he was instituting divorce proceedings.

She lived in a small terrace, Pleasant Place, off Neptune Street, which in those days was much further east than where Burkitt's earlier victims lived. Again it led off the Hessle Road and went down to the railway lines which bordered the Albert Dock. The street was a mixture of industry and dwelling houses, with several factories along it and the Neptune Street Goods Station at the end.

Emma had been living with another fisherman, Thomas Fletcher, when Burkitt became acquainted with her and she continued to see each of them when the other was at sea. It was a situation which again led to frustration on Burkitt's part and once when they were both on shore together he saw Emma and Thomas together in a pub and followed them when they came out. He ran up behind Emma and, coward that he was, struck her in the back. But when Thomas took off his coat to square up to him he ran away.

HULL WOMAN BELIEVED STRANGLED: RIVER RESCUE OF MAN SOUGHT FOR INTERVIEW

Police Find Body in Bed

STARTLING END TO SEARCH FOR TRAWLERHAND

Photocopy from the *Daily Mail* of 1 March 1939. (courtesy of *Hull Daily Mail*)

Burkitt landed in Hull for the last time on Sunday 26 February 1939. The next day he and Emma went out drinking together and seemed to be getting on well. Emma was well known and liked in the area and a fourteen-year-old girl, Peggy Chester, often ran errands for her. She arranged that she and Burkitt would take Peggy to the pictures one afternoon as a treat.

Peggy called round on Tuesday in the afternoon, but Burkitt told her to come back after tea-time. He also gave her an empty bottle and told her to get it filled with aspirins. During the afternoon neighbours heard the unmistakable sounds of quarrelling coming from No. 5 Pleasant Place and Burkitt was seen outside at the end of the terrace shouting, 'I'm fed up with her. She's at it again!' But then he went back inside.

When Peggy came round after tea the door was opened by Burkitt. He looked wild to the young girl as he stood with the hall light behind him. 'I'm sorry Peggy we can't take you tonight, Emma is upstairs asleep.' Then suddenly he switched off the hall light. In the faint light from the kitchen behind, she saw the figure of Burkitt looming up before her and she jumped back in alarm.

'What's the matter, Peggy? Daren't you stay with me in the dark?'

But the frightened young girl turned and rushed away in terror.

About 7.30 a.m. on Wednesday 1 March, Burkitt knocked on the door of his sister's house. She lived with her husband in Witty Street, which in those days ran only between Brighton Street and Scarborough Street. He seemed to be incoherent and neither of them could get any sense out of him. But when her husband had gone to work, Burkitt said, 'I'm dying, I've taken 600 aspirins.' This was obviously an exaggeration, but he was plainly ill. She got him to lie down and was about to go for the doctor, when he jumped up and rushed to the door. 'Goodbye,' he said, 'I've killed Emma and now I'm going to kill myself!'

Burkitt went to trial this time at Leeds Assizes, before Mr Justice Cassels. The prosecution made out a good case for Burkitt being jealous, citing his altercation with Emma and Thomas Fletcher and the words he had used to neighbours. Emma had been found strangled, with the hyoid bone broken in her neck and there were no signs of a struggle – indeed her shoes had been found placed neatly beside the bed. It was obvious that she had been strangled while she was asleep and that the act was premeditated.

But Burkitt went into the witness box and claimed that when they came back from the pub she had jeered at him, naming two other men she had gone with. 'When she said that, everything seemed to go black. When I came round I found I had my hand on her throat. I could not believe it. I had no intention of killing her. I loved her too much for that.'

Incredibly the jury again believed him and brought in a verdict of guilty only to manslaughter. Clearly appalled, the judge addressed Burkitt. 'The jury did not know what you and I know, that this is the third time you have stood in the dock on the charge of murder. Every time it has been for the murder of a woman with whom you have been living. Each time the jury have taken a merciful view. But I can see in your case not one redeeming feature. You will be kept in penal servitude for the rest of your natural life.'

But he wasn't. Although his appeal was dismissed in 1946, he was paroled in 1954 as he was suffering from incurable cancer and died in 1958 at the age of sixty-nine.

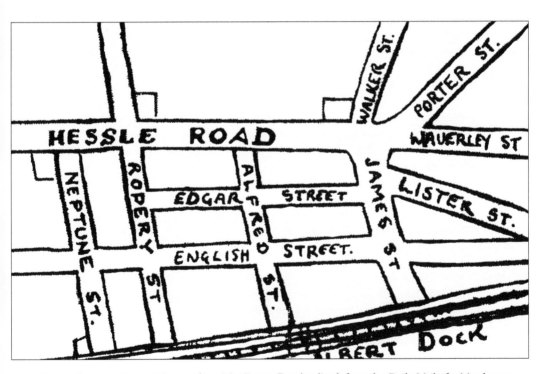

A map showing Neptune Street where Mrs Emma Brookes lived, from the *Daily Mail* of 1 March 1939. (courtesy of *Hull Daily Mail*)

5

Sins of the Son

In 1901 the Grand Theatre stood in George Street, Hull, about midway between Grimston Street and Smeaton Street. Smeaton Street no longer exists and the turning off George Street in that area is now Bond Street. The Grand Theatre had been built in 1893. It was designed by the well-known architect Frank Matcham, who was responsible for many of Hull's theatres, and it opened its doors on 9 January the following year. It was originally called the Grand Opera House, but there were many plays performed there over the years including *The Fanatics, Brewster's Millions, The Right Age to Marry*, and *The Last Waltz*, and of course musicals like *Lilac Time*. William Morton came to Hull from London in March 1895 to take over the Theatre Royal and stayed to buy up many other theatres in the city. He produced the first pantomime in Hull, *The Forty Thieves*; he also bought the Grand.

But the cinema was rapidly overtaking the theatre as a place of popular entertainment. One of the first films shown in the city, a boxing match between Corbett and Fitzsimmons, was shown in 1896 and in the early years of the twentieth century cinemas mushroomed in Hull. At the height of its popularity Hull had thirty-eight picture houses. Inevitably, the Grand Theatre became a cinema. It was renamed the Dorchester and extensive modifications were made. The old three-tier theatre was replaced by a 1,507 seat cinema with only one balcony. In time however, declining audiences forced its closure in 1977 and it was demolished in 1987 and replaced by a bar and shops.

At about a quarter past eleven on the night of Sunday 20 January 1901, fifty-six-year old John Walker and his wife Charlotte left the Grand Theatre by the stage door. They passed into New Garden Street, then into Smeaton Street, Silvester Street, and Bond Street and eventually into Charles Street. John Walker was a cellarman at the theatre and his wife was a dresser there. It took them quite a long time to walk up to Charles Street and to a passer-by it would have quite obvious why: Walker was drunk and staggering about and it was only by hanging on to his wife that he was able to walk reasonably straight at all. Unfortunately, this was not that unusual. The cellarman had ample opportunity to take crafty nips when his boss was not watching. His wife said that beer did not seem to affect him a great deal but whisky sent him mad. And she was in the best position to know. She had only been married to him for four years, but in that time she had suffered numerous beatings and several times he had smashed up the furniture in their small terrace home.

She managed to steer him up Charles Street to Raywell Street and away from the public house on the corner. Then along Raywell Street to one of those small cul-de-sac terraces with which Hull abounded in those days and which ran off at right angles to the main street. The terrace

The Grand Theatre. (courtesy of
Memory Lane)

George Street, Hull

George Street in the early 1900s. (courtesy of Memory Lane)

was called Jarratt's Place and was only a few houses long. But Walker seemed reluctant to go into his house at No. 2 and said that he would go into a barber's shop a few doors along the street. His wife shrugged her shoulders and turned into her own house. She didn't know whether he would be popping into the pub on the corner or going to see the barber whom he knew, but whatever it was, she had no doubt that he would be having a drink before he got home.

When she entered her house she saw her husband's son, who had the same name as his father and who was her stepson. He was talking to a man she knew only as Clark. They chatted together for some time and then Clark left. Soon after, Walker senior arrived home. He glared at his son but said nothing.

Charlotte was preparing a meal. 'Will you have some supper?' she asked her husband.

'No, I'm going to bed', he said and he clumped off up the narrow staircase. Charlotte was quite prepared for his surly behaviour. She knew that father and son did not get on: in fact, that might be too weak an expression. The son, who was only twenty-one, literally hated his father. He complained that his father had thrown him out when he was only a child and he had been forced to live on the street for a period. But she also knew that he was not all that keen on her either, feeling that she had somehow supplanted his mother, whom he adored, even though his mother had since died. And she also realised that the father could not stand the son either. Tensions in the house had been rising for some days now, so she wasn't all that surprised when she heard her husband shouting down the stairs. What did surprise her was when he started making allegations that she had been unfaithful to him with his son.

'God forbid that I should ever do anything of the sort,' she shouted back. But this did not satisfy Walker senior. He continued to make allegations about her and his son in the most vile and objectionable language. And then she heard him staggering down the stairs. He appeared in the kitchen doorway still shouting obscenities and charged across the room at his son. Although he was much older than the boy, he was heavier, and though he was drunk, his charge carried the young man backwards. They swayed about, each fighting for leverage and to land as many blows on each other as they could.

But Charlotte managed to get between them and prise them apart. 'Go back bed John,' she pleaded.

But he threw her off, 'come outside!' He slurred at his son. 'We'll settle this'.

Plainly however he was in no condition to fight, since he could hardly stand upright, and Charlotte got hold of him and turned him towards the stairs. She pushed him up the stairs with difficulty and when he seemed to be going up left him to go back to the kitchen. Walker junior was sitting in a chair when she came in, but he was jumpy and his face was flushed. He got up and pulled open the table drawer and took out a clasp knife, opened it and put it in his jacket pocket.

Walker senior came downstairs again. By this time he was only partly dressed, either having tried to undress himself to get into bed and found he couldn't do it, or deciding that there was more he wanted to say and interrupted his undressing to come down and say it. But he didn't say anything. He lurched into the room and flopped down on a kitchen chair. There he sat breathing heavily. Suddenly he staggered to his feet shouting that he was going to smash all the pictures in the room – smashing furniture seemed to be one of his things.

At this Walker junior jumped to his feet shouting, 'you'll not smash that one'. He pointed to a picture hanging on a wall in the corner of the room, 'that belonged to my dead mother'.

What happened next happened very quickly. As Walker senior lurched forward his son jumped up and pushed his father back on to the chair, drawing the knife at the same time and stabbing him in the chest as he went back. He pulled out the knife and muttered, 'I always said I would do for you'.

Charles Street in the early 1900s. (courtesy of Hull library)

Charlotte screamed as she saw her husband fall forwards with blood gushing from his chest. She grabbed a towel and tried to staunch the blood. Walker junior in a rapid change of mood now kneeled before his father shouting, 'Father! Speak to me!' But his father made no sound other than a groan. 'Forgive me!' pleaded the son, 'forgive me again', but there was no response from the older man. Walker looked up at his stepmother with tears in his eyes. 'My God! What have I done it for?'

Then he rushed out of the little house, but when he heard Charlotte shouting for help he came back inside. By now neighbours were beginning to arrive. They were quite used to hearing quarrels between man and wife, but Charlotte's screaming and shouting this time was something different. Several tried to help her with the injured man and inquired what had happened. When they were told they looked at Walker junior standing wringing his hands in a corner. He could feel their stares upon him and thought that he had better leave, but as he was about to go out, one, a burly lady called Mrs Boasted, grabbed him by the collar.

'No you don't my lad! Someone's gone for the police. You stay here until they get here.'

The young lad stood meekly with Mrs Boasted holding his collar until PC Tanton arrived. He was soon followed by Inspector Kirby, who sent for Dr Close. But by the time the doctor had arrived and examined the stricken man all he could do was to pronounce him dead. Walker was taken to the Norfolk Street police station, only a few streets away, and there he was charged with the murder of his father.

The inquest took place the following day, Monday, at the St Matthias' Mission Room before Col. Thorney. As was common in those days the inquest jury and the witnesses and even the prisoner, John Walker, were invited to view the body. Walker broke down during this procedure. He was in an extremely excitable state and jumped up and made frantic efforts to reach his stepmother. He had to be restrained by police officers. And again during the witnesses' testimony, he several times leaped to his feet to interrupt witnesses. But when he was called, on the advice

Raywell Street today.

of his solicitor Mr Pearlman, he declined to answer questions. The jury had no difficulty in bringing in a verdict of wilful murder against John Aaron Walker, junior.

On the same day Walker was brought before the magistrates in the police court, where Mr Twiss presided. It was the first of many appearances. And on one of these, on Wednesday 6 February, when Deputy Chief Constable Jones asked for a further remand so that the police could complete their inquiries, Mr Pearlman got to his feet. He opposed the remand, saying that they had gone through these farcical proceedings several times already and in the interests of justice a date should be fixed for the proper hearing of the case. It would only be a formality anyway, since he had no doubt that his client would be committed for trial at the assizes. But Mr Pearlman was disappointed. His client was remanded for a further eight days. But on Thursday 14 February the case for the prosecution was finally heard and as Mr Pearlman anticipated, the magistrates committed John Walker for trial at the next assizes at York.

This took place on Thursday 7 March, before Mr Justice Wills. The prosecution was in the hands of Mr Kemp and Walker was defended by Mr Kershaw. The proceedings began at just after eleven o'clock and many witnesses were heard. James Welch, who gave his occupation as an oil miller, said that he was in Raywell Street on Sunday 20 January, when Walker rushed up to him. 'Fetch a policeman and a doctor. I have killed my father!' Welch went inside the house and saw the elder Walker lying on the floor. 'There he is,' said his son. 'I did it because he broke my mother's picture'. Welch then fetched PC Tanton.

Dr Close gave evidence from the post mortem. He said that Walker senior had died from a single stab wound which penetrated an artery and must have been delivered with great force. The most damning evidence, however, came from Charlotte Walker. She said that on the previous Friday night, just before they were going to bed, an argument broke out between father and son and the son shouted at his father, 'I shall do for you. My mother said I was born to be hanged!' Charlotte also said that John Walker junior had only recently been released from prison.

A drawing of John Walker as he appeared in court, taken from the *Hull Times* for 26 January 1901. (courtesy of *Hull Daily Mail*)

She and her husband met her stepson on 11 January when he came out of Hedon Road Jail, after having served several months, and took him home with them. She ended her evidence by describing the events of that tragic Sunday night.

The prosecution closed their case at 2.15 p.m. and soon afterwards Mr Kershaw rose to begin his defence. This was mainly that of provocation, and he claimed that Walker had not intended to kill his father and the whole thing had arisen from the passion of the young man. But in summing up the judge said that insulting words were not sufficient to reduce a charge of murder to manslaughter and that premeditation, the requirement to prove murder, could be an intention of only a few minutes before the blow was struck.

It took the jury just forty minutes to bring in a verdict of guilty, though they did couple it with a strong recommendation to mercy. The judge said he would pass on the recommendation and then donned the black cap for the sentence of death, which would be carried out in Hull. Mr Pearlman immediately appealed against the sentence on the following grounds: the condemned man's youth, provocation, the fact that he had been turned out on to the streets by his father at an early age, and the fact that there had not been an execution in Hull for over a century. Syd Dearnley, who was an assistant executioner during the 1950s, states in his autobiography *The Hangman's Tale* that in his opinion there was no logic in the giving of reprieves and often they seemed to be aimed at local communities, either to placate them or to warn them. Whether that was so in this case will never be known, but what is known is that the reprieve was granted within three days of it being received and John Walker was sentenced to life imprisonment.

6

The Power of Dreams

The town of Scarborough is some forty miles north of Hull and like Hull it is an important fishing port as well as being one of the most popular holiday resorts on the East Coast. Traces of Stone Age and Bronze Age settlers have been found in the area and the Romans built a signal station on the Scarborough Headland, but there is no evidence that they used it much. The first proof of substantial settlement in the area comes from the Vikings, and they gave the town its name. A Viking nicknamed *Skarthi*, which means 'harelip', decided to settle there and the place became known as Skarthi's Burgh or Skarthi's Stronghold. It received its first charter from Henry I in 1100 and the first castle was built in 1136. Scarborough soon became a major fishing port and when Edward I visited the town in 1275 it was decreed that no rival port should be allowed between Scarborough and the Humber. The town has had its share of bloodshed: it was attacked by the Scots under Robert the Bruce and became part of the Peasants Revolt in 1380, and the castle was besieged during the Pilgrimage of Grace in 1536.

During the Elizabethan and Stuart times the town began to decline in importance, but around 1625 a Mrs Farrow, the wife of a town bailiff, discovered a small spring below the cliff which seemed to have medicinal properties and the place over the years became a spa town. The spa was later destroyed by an earthquake, but by then Scarborough had became a holiday town and in the Victoria era, with its two extensive beaches, it became one of the premier sea-bathing towns on the east coast.

Like all major seaside resorts it became a magnet for crooks and conmen and in 1920s a certain Ernest Dyer went there. But this is to anticipate the story. The case actually began far to the south, in Sydenham, Buckinghamshire. During the late summer of 1922 Mrs Tombe, the wife of the Revd Tombe, was sitting one morning having breakfast in the rectory with her husband. She had been silent through most of the meal, but then over the toast and marmalade she looked up at him with tears in her eyes.

'Gordon, I had that dream again last night!'

The Revd Tombe leaned forward and took his wife's hand. 'Was it the same as before?'

'No, I did see Eric again, but this time –', she stopped and reached for her handkerchief and dabbed at her streaming eyes and it was some time before she could continue, 'Gordon, I think he was dead! I think I saw his body at the bottom of a well!'

Their son, Eric Gordon Tombe, was twenty-eight. He had been an artillery officer in the First World War and was a young man of independent means, but his parents had not seen or

Eric Tombe from the *Daily Sketch* for 14 September 1923. (courtesy of the Solo Syndication/Associated Newspapers Ltd)

heard from him for several months. His father had written to an accommodation address Eric used in Jermyn Street in London, but the managers of the letter drop had not seen him either since April. The Revd Tombe advertised in London papers asking for information about his son, but he received no replies. Then he went up to London himself and made enquiries in the Haymarket area, where Eric had had a flat, going from shop to shop and asking if anyone had seen or heard anything of his son. At a barber's shop the proprietor remembered Eric ('the lieutenant', he called him), but he didn't know where he was and he hadn't seen him for some time. But just as the reverend was leaving, he called him back.

'I've just remembered. I've seen him with another ex-officer. A chap called Dyer, I think it was. A bit of a shady character I thought he was. I think they were in partnership in a stud farm, somewhere, but I'm not sure where.'

The Revd Tombe had never heard of this venture and he didn't know who Dyer was. But all the same he was uneasy about what he had heard and in view of his wife's persistent dreams about their son he decided to go to Scotland Yard. There he saw Superintendent Francis Carlin. He put all the information he had obtained before the superintendent and told him of his wife's dreams. Carlin promised to do what he could and began an investigation.

Ernest Dyer from the *Daily Sketch* for 14 September 1923. (courtesy of Solo Syndication/Associated Newspapers Ltd)

He discovered that Ernest Dyer was a year older than Eric Tombe. Dyer had been born of poor parents in Brighton and had started his career as a gas-fitter's mate. He immigrated to Australia when he was seventeen and in 1914 joined the Australian Army and was wounded at Gallipoli. When he recovered he was commissioned in the Royal West Surreys and transferred later to the Royal Artillery. It was when he and Eric were working in the Air Ministry after the war that they met.

In July 1920 Dyer persuaded Eric to go into partnership with him in a stud farm at Kenley, near Croydon, called The Welcomes. Although Eric put up most of the money to buy the place Dyer, his wife and family – he had two children – lived in the farm house, while Eric rented a cottage nearby in Dorking. Dyer insisted on taking out fire insurance on the farm and then paid the first premium himself. But the stud farm was not a success, mainly because Dyer spent very little time at the place and much more at race meetings where he lost a great deal of money. After about a year a fire broke out at The Welcomes, which destroyed many of the buildings. But after an inspection the insurance company were suspicious of the cause of the fire and refused to pay up. Dyer didn't pursue the matter and the partnership with Tombe broke up.

Eric Tombe seemed to have disappeared round about April 1922. His mother had a letter from him at about that time saying that he was going to Paris for a few days and during that month his bank received a communication from him transferring some of the balance of his account to the Paris branch. On 25 April the bank received a letter apparently signed by Eric Tombe asking the bank to allow his business partner Ernest Dyer to draw on the account. The bank authorised this and Dyer began to substantially reduce the account. Then on 7 August the Paris branch wrote to the London office saying that Dyer had come into the bank with a power of attorney, apparently again signed by Eric, asking for the balance of the account to be transferred to Paris. This was again agreed to and the account was rapidly emptied. After that cheques appeared in hotels, restaurants and shops around England, apparently signed by Eric Tombe, but they could not be honoured because the account was empty.

Carlin also found two girlfriends of Eric Tombe's. Their names were never revealed and I shall call them Cynthia and Jane. Cynthia had been in contact with Eric in early April. She told him that she was going to stay with some friends in the North and he agreed to meet her off the train at Euston when she returned. But when she arrived at the London station it wasn't Eric who stood on the platform, but Ernest Dyer.

'What are you doing here Ernest? Where's Eric?'

Dyer handed her a telegram that he said he had received from Eric saying that that he had had to go overseas suddenly.

Cynthia read the telegram through carefully. 'This doesn't sound like Eric. He would never say 'overseas', he would say Paris or Rome.'

'I can assure you —.'

'Do you know what I think Ernest? I think you wrote that telegram yourself.'

Dyer's face went white. 'You're a clever girl Cynthia, but I can assure you it's all right. Eric did ask me to write that. He had to dash off to the continent in a hurry and he asked me to write the telegram and meet you.' He picked up her case and they began to walk along the platform.

'I'm still not happy about this,' she said.

'Look, I've got to dash off now. But I'll come and see you in a few days time.'

'Come and see me tonight.'

'Well I don't know if I can —.'

'Come and see me tonight or I'll go to the police.'

It was a much chastened Dyer who turned up at Cynthia's flat that night. And he was taken aback when he saw that she had two burly young men with her. 'Don't be afraid, Ernest. They are only friends of Eric and myself. And they are here only to give me some advice. I had a letter from Eric only last week. The one where he said he would meet me at Euston. He also said that he was going to see you at The Welcomes.'

'Yes that's quite true.'

'But I thought the place had burnt down.'

'Most of it, yes. But my wife and family are still living in part of the stables that didn't get damaged. That was the last time I actually saw Eric. It was Thursday of last week. We'd been talking about getting back into partnership.'

Superintendent Carlin on the right and Inspector Hedges on the left from the *Daily Sketch* for 14 September 1923. (courtesy of Solo Syndication/Associated Newspapers Ltd)

Cynthia looked doubtful. 'Eric told me he had broken off with you because he didn't think you were, well, quite honest.'

Dyer laughed uneasily. 'It was all a misunderstanding. But Eric definitely came to see me. In fact we had quite a long evening together and it went on so late that he missed the last bus and we had to walk to Croydon. I put him on the last bus to London and that's the last I saw of him.'

Cynthia still looked doubtful. And she didn't say anything for a long time. Then she said slowly. 'You know what I think? I think you might have done away with him. And unless you can convince me otherwise I'm going to go to the police.'

Dyer jumped as if one of the burly young men had got up and hit him. He cowered away. 'If you do that Cynthia, I might as well blow my brains out. You know my reputation is so bad after that business of the fire that nobody will believe me.' His head sank on to his chest. Then he raised it looked directly at her. 'All I can do is to betray the best friend I've ever had. Eric has gone off with another girl!'

'I don't believe it!'

'It's true! It's true!' He made a dash for the door as one of the young men jumped up. But he was not quick enough as the man got between him and the door. 'It's true!' He turned to face them again. 'You can ask anybody! Ask the porter at his flat in the Haymarket. He's seen them together!'

A look of doubt appeared on Cynthia's face.

'I'm sorry,' babbled Dyer. 'I didn't want to upset you, but he told me they were going off together. I don't know where.' He began to edge backwards towards the door. And then as his audience stood transfixed he made his escape, shouting as he went through the door. 'I do know that they're engaged!'

Eric Tombe did have another girlfriend. As with Cynthia, her name was never revealed and I shall call her Jane. She said that she had been going out with Eric for about a year, she knew Dyer, and the last time she saw Eric he told her that he was going to The Welcomes the next day to see Dyer. He said that he would see her the next day at his flat in the Haymarket. When she turned up the next day she let herself into the flat, since she had a key, and found a telegram from Eric on the mat inside the front door. He said that he would be going away for a few days and would be writing to her. Soon after this the telephone rang. It was Dyer and he was enquiring if Eric had got home all right. They had had quite a drinking session last night, he said, and he had put Eric on a bus for London. Later that day he arrived looking very much the worse for wear, and said that he would spend the night in Eric's flat.

Jane went home, but came back the next day to find Dyer busily putting Eric's clothes into a big trunk. He told her that Eric had instructed him to give up the flat and he paid the outstanding rent with a cheque taken from Eric's cheque book. It seems that Jane was not made of such stern stuff as Cynthia, because she meekly accepted this and never saw or heard from Eric Tombe again.

By this time Superintendent Carlin was convinced that Dyer had murdered his partner and had looted his bank account. But where was the body? It was a fair guess that it was somewhere at The Welcomes stud farm and if Mrs Tombe's dreams were anything to go by, the first place to look was in any wells there might be there. He obtained a large-scale map of the area and discovered that there were five wells located on the property.

It was a day in late September 1923 that Superintendent Francis Carlin, together with DI Hedges of the Z Division of the Metropolitan Police and the local division that included Kenley, arrived at the five-bar gate at the entrance to The Welcomes. When they got into the farm they found the place derelict and overgrown with weeds. With the aid of the map Carlin was able to locate the wells. But they were all filled in and the squad of policemen, in rubber

Fire-charred ruins of The Welcomes from the *Daily Sketch* for 14 September 1923. Inset is the Revd Gordon Tombe. (courtesy of Solo Syndication/Associated Newspapers Ltd)

boots and in their shirt sleeves, had the unenviable task of clearing out the bricks, slabs of broken concrete and general building debris, not to mention the vegetation, which now choked the pits. It was back-breaking work with their picks and shovels, but they had finally cleared two and found nothing in either.

By this time it was getting dark and DI Hedges, seeing that the men were tired, asked Carlin if they could stop now, and carry on tomorrow.

'I want this third one cleared,' said the obstinate Carlin.

So with the aid of lanterns and after a brief rest they started on the third. It was deeper than the others and a man had to go down eventually on a rope to clear away the last remnants of rubbish near the bottom. But eventually there came a shout from the man on the rope. And all the men at the top leaned over, shining their lanterns into the pit. And there sticking out from a pile of stones they could see a human foot.

The Revd Gordon Tombe was able to identify his son's body by a wristwatch inscribed with the words 'E. Gordon Tombe', a gold safety pin and a silk scarf, all belonging to his son. And when Mrs Dyer was interviewed by the police she remembered a night when she and her children were living at The Welcomes and she heard a strange noise from outside, like stones rattling. Since her husband was away she was frightened and went outside cautiously with their dog by her side. In the darkness she could just make out the figure of Dyer.

'Ernest? Is that you? I thought you were abroad.'

'Keep your voice down! You know I can't be seen around here in daylight, after that business of the fire.'

Detectives searching a well at The Welcomes from the *Daily Sketch* for 14 September 1923. (courtesy of Solo Syndication/Associated Newspapers Ltd)

Mrs Dyer from the *Daily Sketch* for
14 September 1923. (courtesy of Solo
Syndication/Associated Newspapers Ltd)

She wondered afterwards what he had been doing, for he was very secretive and would tell her nothing. Now it seemed pretty obvious.

On a cold and windy day in November, DI Abbot of the Scarborough Constabulary approached a bulky man standing on the edge of the pavement in Bar Street, Scarborough. 'Is your name Fitzsimmons?'

The man looked round. 'Yes it is. What's it got to do with you?'

The detective produced his warrant card. 'I'd like to have a word with you if I may. Is there somewhere where we can talk?'

The man pointed behind him to the building he had just left. It was the Old Bar Hotel and stood just beyond where there used to be the old toll bar in the street. They went inside the hotel and the man pointed to a lounge. 'We can go in there.' The room was empty and they stood by the fire.

'Now can you tell me what this is all about?' asked Fitzsimmons.

What it was actually all about, was that a man who called himself Fitzsimmons had inserted an advertisement in the *Scarborough Evening News* and the *Scarborough Daily Post*. It read, 'wanted a few gentlemen of highest integrity as agents; no capital required. Apply Fitzsimmons Old Bar Hotel'.

Since this wasn't that long after the end of the First World War there were a few ex-servicemen with gratuities from their war service, but no jobs. But those that had applied found that far from offering them jobs, Fitzsimmons seemed keener on trying to get them to invest money in various schemes he was running. And some of them complained to the police. In addition, a man named Fitzsimons was suspected of passing dud cheques in various hotels in the North.

'I wonder if you can identify yourself?' asked the inspector.

Fitzsimmons went into a long explanation, saying that he was the son of an important businessman who was a JP in Carlisle and he was travelling on behalf of his father. And although he gave an address in Butcher-gate, Carlisle, he couldn't give a telephone number for the business, claiming that his father didn't like telephones.

'I'll tell you what sir. We'll go down to the police station while you think about it. When we are there I'll make some enquiries of the Carlisle police and we'll be able to clear this matter up quickly.'

At this point another police officer entered the room. 'This is Detective Constable Nalton,' introduced the inspector. 'This gentleman is coming to the station with us', he told the constable. 'Would you go to the proprietress and ask her to pack this gentleman's bag for him.'

'I'm quite capable of packing my own bag.'

'Just as you like sir. We'll follow you up to your room.'

Fitzsimmons hesitated for a moment. Then he shrugged his shoulders and led the way upstairs. When they reached the first landing, with Fitzsimmons in the lead, the inspector suddenly saw the man turn and his left hand went to his pocket. Suspecting that he might have a gun, the inspector and the constable closed on him and fell on top of the struggling man. Suddenly a shot rang out and the man stopped struggling. When they turned him over they saw that he had indeed a revolver in his hand and one chamber had been fired. By the time the doctor and ambulance arrived the man was dead.

A subsequent search of his room turned up some cheques on which the name Eric Tombe had been pencilled in, obviously for inking in later on. And two service medals were found, on the back of which were stamped the words 'Lieutenant E. Dyer.' But the incredible thing was that this happened on 16 November 1922, ten months before the body of Eric Tombe was discovered!

7

Calypso Killer

In the 1930s the area south of Paragon station, Hull, was a maze of little streets. The main artery was the Anlaby Road and south of this a tramway ran up from the Hessle Road, through Porter Street and on to the Anlaby Road by way of Midland Street. The turning on the right just before you got to Anlaby Road, and where the tramway also branched right, is Osborne Street. The first turning on the right along Osborne Street in those days was Upper Union Street. It was only a short street leading down to Great Passage Street and it had a pub on the corner with Osborne Street, the Drum and Cymbals.

At No. 7 Upper Union Street lived Theresa May Hemstock, who was forty-seven, but still attractive enough for her current beau who was a forty-nine-year-old West Indian seaman. George Emmanuel Michael was of Danish nationality and was registered in Hull as an alien. In addition he was a black man and although big ports like Hull would be full of different nationalities, at that time black men would not be all that common.

Theresa Hemstock lived with George Michael in Upper Union Street, at least while he was not at sea. When he was she probably had other lovers as well. And as with many seamen and their partners their relationship was a rocky one. Michael was a passionate and a violent man and there were constant quarrels and reconciliations. Possibly he wanted a more stable relationship; or maybe he wanted to pin Theresa down to a more permanent state. At all events he managed to persuade her to get married and they were united in wedlock, if precious little else, on 23 November 1929, at the registry office on Anlaby Road.

The only trouble was that Theresa was already married. She had been married many years ago, but had not lived with her husband for well over twenty years. They had not been divorced and he was still alive and living in Hull. She did not tell Michael that however; she said she was a widow. Her husband, she told him, had been a soldier, but had since died. Whether Michael believed her is not known, but they lived together for three years. Then Theresa decided to make the break. It might have been an attack of conscience or more likely she saw it as a means of getting rid of him and his violent behaviour. On 12 December 1931, supported by her cousin Louisa Hoult, she went to the police and confessed her bigamy to DS Howgate. Michael was told of this by the sergeant when he returned from sea and he was furious. 'She's done this just to get rid of me! But I'm not afraid, I'll kill her!'

Michael left No. 7 Upper Union Street and went into lodgings with a Mrs Minnie Morrison at No. 9 Providence Row, Walker Street, another street which used to link Anlaby Road and Hessle Road. A friend of his, Charles Steede, another black seaman, also lived there.

The Drum and Cymbals public house where the licensee heard Michael shouting. (courtesy of Hull Library)

HULL MURDER CHARGE

COLOURED MAN WHO LOVED DEAD WOMAN MOST OF ALL

SENT FOR TRIAL

WEAPON TURNED ON HIMSELF WHEN PARTED BY POLICE

THE terrible scene which led to the New Year's Eve tragedy in Upper Union-st. was described to the Hull Stipendiary Magistrate on Thursday, when George Emmanuel Michael, aged 49, a coloured man, of Providence-terrace, Walker-street, was charged with the wilful murder of Theresa Mary Hemstock, a married woman, of 7, Upper Union-street, Hull.

A constable who was in the house with the two said that Michael rushed at the woman with a dagger and landed several blows about her head and shoulders before he could be separated from her.

Then he drove the dagger into his own left side.

Witnesses stated that Michael, who time after time said he loved Hemstock, had accused her of being unfaithful to him, and said he would go to the gallows for her.

Photocopy of a portion of *The Hull Times* for 20 February 1932. (courtesy of *Hull Daily Mail*)

One evening in late December Michael and Mrs Morrison were playing cards in the kitchen, when he asked her, 'Minnie, do you think it wicked to kill anyone?'

'I certainly do!'

'Suppose they do something bad to you?'

'It's still not right to kill them. And in any case if you do, you yourself will be killed.'

This led on to a discussion of hanging. 'They do not hang people in Denmark,' said Michael.

'Well they do here, unless it can be proved to be an accident.'

Michael was silent for some time. But presumably Mrs Morrison knew all about Theresa Hemstock, for she said gently, 'you'll get over it in time.'

'I shall never get over it. I love that woman!' But he couldn't resist the temptation to rail against Theresa. 'She's been unfaithful to me you know. I found out that she had another man living with her when I was not there.'

'Perhaps he was just another lodger.'

'Oh no. He wasn't, I know they were sleeping together.'

'Well that's up to her. She's a free agent isn't she?'

'No she isn't. She married me. Mind you I found out that she was married already and her husband is still alive. She's had all my money as well.'

There seemed little more to be said, but plainly Michael was still seething with resentment. Just after Christmas, on the last day of the old year, he went into a shop on the Hessle Road and bought a knife and a sheath for it. It must be said though that afterwards the shopkeeper could not identify Michael as the man who bought it, but he did identify the sheath because it had a special mark on it.

That same day in the afternoon Charles Steede, who had earlier lit a fire in the living room, noticed that somebody had put what looked like a screwed up rag on the blaze. As he thought it would prevent the fire burning properly he pulled it off. It was only smouldering and it quickly went out after he took it off the fire. Inside he found some filings. He looked about for Michael to ask him if he had put it on the fire, but couldn't find him. He then looked in Michael's room and noticed a file on a chair and also a bottle of red ink.

Mrs Mary Harold lived at No. 5 Upper Union Street, next door to Theresa Hemstock. Later that same afternoon when she was in her kitchen at the rear of the house she heard the sound of breaking glass. She looked out of the window and saw Michael, whom she knew, standing at the back of Theresa's house and his hand was bleeding. He was shouting for Theresa to come out. Mrs Harold summed up the situation and went out of her front door. She knocked on her next-door neighbour's front door and called to Theresa to come out and shelter in her house. And this Theresa did, just managing to get inside before Michael hurtled round to the front to intercept her. But he guessed where she had gone and began banging on Mrs Harold's door telling her to send Theresa out to him.

'She's not here!'

'Yes she is!'

Mrs Harold, who was a resourceful woman, thought things over. She knew it would be difficult to get rid of Michael and he might start breaking her windows as well. 'You go and fetch a policeman and then you can come in and see her.'

'Tell her to come out. I won't do anything to her.' But then rage overcame him. 'By God!' he shouted. 'I'll go to the gallows for her before I leave this ★★★★★★★ street!'

At the end of the street, just a few yards away, was the Drum and Cymbals public house. The licensee, Thomas Thornton, could hear the shouting in the street outside; in fact he heard the last words that Michael used. He turned to one of his customers, Frederick Baxter, and sent him off for a policeman. Then he armed himself with a heavy staff and stood ready by the front door of the pub.

St Andrew's Dock in about 1920 showing a steam trawler being unloaded. (courtesy of Memory Lane)

PC Peam, who had been in the Anlaby Road, eventually arrived in Upper Union Street. He saw Michael in the street and asked him what the trouble was. 'That woman in there,' he pointed to Mrs Harold's house, 'has my naturalisation papers, and won't give them to me.' This was a lie of course. Michael had no naturalisation papers, since he was a registered alien. But the policeman did not know that, and neither, it seems, did Theresa Hemstock. She came out of Mrs Harold's house and told the officer that she did not have the papers. But PC Peam, who had probably come across similar situations before, said, 'if you have the papers you must give them to him.'

'I haven't got them!' She shouted, 'look, come inside and I'll show you what he's been up to!' She led the way into No. 7, down the passage and towards the back door, followed by the police officer and Michael. 'Look at that,' she said, 'he did that just this afternoon.' Both glass panels of the back door, top and bottom, were broken.

'Did you do that?'

'Yes I did, but she wouldn't let me in', and he repeated his accusation that she had his papers.

'I haven't got his damn papers. Look, I'll show you.' She went upstairs and came down with a box of papers which she emptied on to a nearby couch. She rooted through them watched by the policeman. 'They're not there. I haven't got them.'

'She's lying. She's hidden them.' But perhaps realising that this was end of the farce he pushed the policeman aside and sprang at Theresa, swinging his right arm and catching her a blow to the head. PC Peam jumped after him and grabbed him by the collar, but he could not stop the ferocity of Michael's attack on the woman. Then he realised that Michael had a knife in his right hand and was landing blows to the woman's head and shoulders with it. He pulled Michael and tried to grab his arm, but the maniacal fury of the seaman was so great he could not prevent the blows falling. Just then Thomas Thornton rushed in carrying his heavy stave and hit Michael several times over the head with it until the seaman collapsed on the floor. But just before he went down he thrust the dagger into his left side. Theresa was screaming and her head and shoulders were covered in blood. Then she too collapsed.

Both Theresa and Michael were taken to the Royal Infirmary. But when Dr Eric Gillespie the house surgeon examined Theresa he saw that she was dead. He afterwards said that there were six deep wounds in the woman's body, mostly in the region of the left shoulder. He was of the

Hull Prison in the 1930s, where George Michael was hanged. (courtesy of Hull library)

opinion that death had occurred due to haemorrhage from the wound which had penetrated the apex of a lung. Michael had suffered a wound to the left breast and another to the top of his head. He was seen soon after he was brought in by DI Smith and said to him; 'I told you what I would do to her if she was unfaithful.'

Michael remained in hospital for several weeks recovering from his wounds. But eventually he was discharged and on 9 February he was charged with the murder of Theresa Hemstock. It was only then that he discovered that she was dead. The inspector found among Michael's belongings a pocket book in which he had written in red ink:

I am writing on behalf of the police of Hull and to give a clear statement of my present state of mind. I have signed it myself. I now decide to pay the penalty for the beastly things this woman has done to me. My brain feels as if there are many worms turning up and down in my head, so I have decided to go out of it. I have been forced in marriage to this woman.

Then she has misconducted herself on many occasions and the last of all after taking the whole of my earnings sent me out of the house which I have provided for her many years now. I am in misery and so ashamed of her actions that I am blinded out of reason. Hoping to be forgiven by the Heavenly Master for my grievance is more than I can stand for.

Michael was brought before the Hull magistrates on 20 February and after evidence had been presented, he was committed for trial at Leeds Assizes on 4 March 1932, before Mr Justice Humphreys. Mr Arthur Morley led for the prosecution and Michael was defended by Mr Willoughby-Jardine KC. Premeditation was easily shown by Michael's statement in red ink, clearly written before the murder, the purchase of the knife and the various statements he had made to people he knew. No evidence was called by the defence, but defending counsel submitted that at the time Michael was not responsible for his actions. The judge in his summing up said that for this to be so the defence must prove in evidence that the man did not know what he was doing.

The jury took only fifty-five minutes to bring in a verdict of guilty, and the sentence of death was passed. On Wednesday 27 April 1932 George Emmanuel Michael was hanged at the Hedon Road Prison, Hull; the sentence being carried out by Thomas Pierrepoint, assisted by Henry Pollard.

8

'My God! What has he been doing to you?'

It was about just after four o'clock in the afternoon of Friday 22 July 1898, when the couple arrived. They knocked on the door of No. 1 Princes Row, a turning off Dock Street in Hull, and it was opened by an elderly German lady, Mrs Elizabeth Shikoffsky. She looked the couple up and down. They were both in their thirties. She was short and was wearing a reddish coloured blouse and a dark skirt, the usual length for those times, nearly dragging on the ground, and a white sailor hat with a black band round it. She was obviously drunk, leaning her head on the man's shoulder. He looked pleasant enough and was wearing a dark suit and a bowler hat. He was carrying a case in one hand and a folded coat over his arm.

'I'm sorry to trouble you,' he said, 'but I believe you do let rooms. Could we have a room for a couple of hours? We have been travelling and my wife is feeling tired.'

The German lady nodded. 'You'll have to pay in advance,' she said promptly.

The man put his hand into his inside pocket and pulled out a well-filled wallet. When he had handed over the money the landlady showed them into an upstairs room. Then she went back downstairs. At about half past five the man clattered back down the stairs. Mrs Shikoffsky hearing him came quickly out of one of the downstairs rooms. 'Where is your wife?' she enquired.

'She wants a little more rest. I'll be back in a few minutes.'

But the man did not come back.

Mrs Shikoffsky waited an hour or so and then went upstairs to their room. The woman was lying on top of the bed, fully clothed and her hat was on a nearby table. She appeared to be asleep. According to the landlady she waited a little while longer to see if the woman's husband would return and when he didn't she went back upstairs again. This time she shook the woman awake and asked her if she was all right. The woman, who said her name was Emily Hall, asked Mrs Shikoffsky if she would help to loosen her corset. The landlady helped her to pull up her skirt and then she saw the blood: pools of it on the bed and on the floor.

'My God! What has he been doing to do you?'

'The ******* has done plenty!'

Emily Hall was thirty-seven years old. Her father William Hall had been a carver and a guilder, but he had died many years before. She had a sister, Charlotte, who worked as a domestic servant at St George's House, Anlaby Road and they saw each other fairly frequently. Charlotte was under the impression that Emily was married to a Mr George, who was a stableman employed by Messrs Wing, cab proprietors, of Baker Street. But he said that he only employed her as a housekeeper at No. 14 Clarendon Terrace, Clarendon

Drawing of Elizabeth Shikoffsky from the *Daily Mail* for 9 August 1898. (courtesy of *Hull Daily Mail*).

Street. He had done so for five years, but she had been increasingly beset by a drink problem and would frequently go out at night and return home drunk. She had left in the June of the previous year.

She then went to live with a widow, a Mrs Leticia Ann Hunt, at No. 8 Poplar Crescent, Westbourne Street, but there her pattern of behaviour continued. She frequently went out and returned drunk. This she had done on the Thursday, the day before her encounter with the man with the dark suit and the bowler hat, coming home about 11.45 p.m. under the influence of drink. She went out again the next day at about midday, having drunk a cup of tea and a pennyworth of beer, and finished up at the house off Dock Street.

When Mrs Shikoffsky saw all the blood (there was even a bowl containing blood on the wash stand and a towel soaked in it) she panicked and rushed next door to her niece, Amelia Wendt. She told her niece what had happened and sent her off to a pharmacy in Lowgate to see if she could get anything for the woman. But Amelia returned to say the pharmacist wouldn't give her anything without a doctor's prescription.

The landlady went back upstairs to Emily Hall. 'You'll have to go. I can't cope with you here.'

'Oh, leave me until tomorrow. I shall be all right.'

Mrs Shikoffsky came downstairs and said to her niece, 'See if you can get hold of George Sykes and see if you can find a cab.'

Drawing of George Stoner from the *Daily Mail* for 25 July 1898. (courtesy of *Hull Daily Mail*)

The young woman went off and returned with George Sykes, who was a friend of theirs and lived nearby. After some discussion with the two women he went upstairs and carried Emily down in his arms to the cab waiting outside. Then he and Amelia Wendt accompanied her to the infirmary. By this time Emily was moaning with pain.

Mr C.V. Knight, assistant house surgeon at the infirmary, first saw Emily at about a quarter past ten on that Friday evening. But there was little that he could do except to try and stem the bleeding. In those days blood transfusions were unheard of. Emily Hall died at five minutes past twelve that night.

The post-mortem was conducted on Saturday by Dr Hainsworth, assisted by Mr Knight. The injuries were so horrific that when they were due to be reported at the committal proceedings, the deputy chief constable ordered all women to leave the court, although the newspapers at the time reported that many were seen to leave with disappointment on their faces. The two doctors were of the opinion that her injuries, which could not have been self inflicted, had been caused by something having been thrust inside her, possibly a hand, with considerable violence. A bar of soap was discovered high up inside her body. And they both agreed that the injuries were the cause of death. In view of the fact that the injuries would have caused her considerable pain they suggested that she might have been in such a state of intoxication, or under the influence of some drug, that she might not have cried out.

Between about half past two and three o'clock on the Friday, Fred Inkson, who was the son of the landlord of the Flower Pot, in Whitefriargate, was serving customers in the bar. He saw a man he knew come into the snug with a woman and another man. The man he knew was George Stoner and he was wearing a dark suit. The woman had on a reddish coloured blouse and a white sailor hat with a black band around it. Stoner, who seemed in a good mood, ordered a glass of beer for himself, a whisky for the woman and a brandy for the other man. They could be seen from the smoke room and a voice came from there. 'Hullo George, I see you're at the game again!'

Stoner laughed, 'Come round here and have a drink. You can have anything you like except champagne! I had a good day yesterday. Backed 'Dinna Forget' which came home in a canter.' The three stayed only about a quarter of an hour and then left.

Later that afternoon Frederick Clifford was in the Theatre Tavern in Dock Street when two men and a woman came in. The pub was small and dark and lit by gaslight, but he recognised one of the men, George Stoner, as he knew him very well. He also knew the woman by sight

Photocopy of a portion of the *Daily Mail* for 25 July 1898. (courtesy of *Hull Daily Mail*)

although he didn't know her name. But he didn't know the other man. Stoner appeared very jovial and was buying everyone drinks which he paid for with a sovereign, but Clifford couldn't hear any conversation the three had. Eventually Stoner and the woman left together leaving the other man behind.

About just after four that afternoon Robert Saunders was standing outside the premises where he worked in Dock Street. He was a foreman employed by Mr T.M. Roberts, an oil merchant, at No. 24 Dock Street and lived over the premises. Saunders was standing by the front door when he saw George Stoner (whom he knew as 'Stoney') approaching from the direction of the Theatre Tavern, and a woman with a reddish coloured blouse with dark spots on it and a dark skirt. He nodded knowingly at Stoner as they passed and said, 'you'll be all right there Stoney.' Stoner looked round and laughed. Then the couple turned into Princes Row, which was only about 15 yards from the T.M. Roberts' front door.

The next night, Saturday, Saunders was in the Baltic Tavern, in Dock Street, at about half past six, when he heard some men talking about the death of a woman who had gone into a house in Princes Row with a man the previous day. He told the landlord of the pub what he had seen and the landlord got in touch with the police. Saunders was interviewed by Superintendent Emerson and Sgt Alvin and repeated his story. He was taken by the police to the infirmary where he was shown the body of the dead woman. He said he thought it might be the woman he had seen with Stoner, but when he was shown the blouse and skirt she had been wearing he unhesitatingly identified them as being those the woman had been wearing the previous afternoon.

Saunders was also able to help the police in another way. He pointed out that Stoner often

Dock Street today. A turning off here was Princes Row where Stoner and Emily Hall went for their tragic assignation.

used the Alhambra Hotel in Carr Lane and he offered to go there that night with the police and identify Stoner if he came in. So that evening Saunders went to the pub, leaving Sgt Hotham and Sgt Alvin outside. Stoner was already there, this time wearing a light coloured suit. Saunders began talking to him: then, when Stoner was about to leave, Saunders said he would come with him. They came out of the pub together and at the corner of Paragon Street and Chariot Street, Saunders nodded at the two policemen. Sgt Hotham stepped forward and arrested Stoner.

George Stoner, whose age was given as thirty-five, lived at No. 72 Peel Street, which is off Spring Bank. He came from a highly respected family in Hull who had been involved in the public-house business in the High Street. A well-known character in the town, Stoner had been an engraver, a bicycle manufacturer and a commission agent. In the days of the 'penny farthing' bicycle, Stoner had been a noted performer and had won many races at the Old Botanic Gardens track. He was married and had two children. He had been separated from his wife, but recently there had been a reconciliation and they were now living together. Indeed, when his wife was interviewed by the press when Stoner had been charged with murder she said was positive that her husband was innocent and would have no difficulty establishing an alibi.

After being arrested Stoner was taken to the police station in Parliament Street. He was there placed in a line up of five other men and viewed by Mrs Elizabeth Shikoffsky, who identified him as the man she had seen with the woman on the previous Friday. Stoner was then charged by Sgt Hotham with the murder of Emily Hall. Sgt Hotham subsequently made a search of Stoner's house. In a back bedroom he found a suit of black clothes and a linen shirt. There were stains – afterwards proved to be blood by Mr J. Baynes, borough analyst – on the right wrist of

Carr Lane in the early 1900s, where Stoner was arrested. (courtesy of Memory Lane)

the shirt and down the front. Blood was also found on the right-hand pocket of the trousers and a white handkerchief found in the pocket of the jacket. But at that time it was impossible to say if the blood was human or not.

The trial took place at the York Assizes on Wednesday 30 November 1898, before Mr Justice Darling. The prosecution was in the hands of Mr Meek and he presented witnesses to show that Stoner had been seen with a woman answering the description of Emily Hall both before and after going into No. 1 Princes Row. Blood was found on his clothes, though it could not be proved to be human, but it all added up to a strong circumstantial case. The medical evidence clearly appalled everybody in court and, it would have been thought, must have had considerable influence on the jury.

The defence was a curious one. Mr Mellor called no witnesses, not even Stoner himself, and because of this when the prosecuting counsel had finished his summing up, Mr Mellor was allowed to be the last to speak. He concentrated almost entirely on arguing that it wasn't Stoner who committed the deed – yet he offered no alibi for his client, merely asserting that the prosecution case hadn't been proved.

Mr Justice Darling in his summing up pointed out that if the prisoner had acted at the instigation of the deceased then there was one person who could throw light upon it and that was the prisoner. Yet he had not been called. If the deceased consented to the prisoner doing something to her, but he went a great deal further than she desired, he would be guilty of a misdemeanour and that would be manslaughter. But if he did that which a reasonable man must have known would have caused grievous bodily harm, then that would be a felony and he would be guilty of murder.

THE INFIRMARY.

HULL.

The infirmary in the early 1900s, where Emily Hall was taken. (courtesy of Memory Lane)

The jury retired at a quarter past five, but they were back within half an hour with the verdict 'guilty of committing grievous bodily harm, but without premeditation.' The judge protested that this was no verdict at all and sent them back. After a long wait they returned to ask the judge a question and Mr Justice Darling repeated the conditions he had outlined in his summing up. The jury retired again and after ten minutes returned with a verdict of guilty of murder, but with a recommendation to mercy.

The judge passing sentence said that the case was one in which 'the circumstances are almost too revolting for words. I cannot for a moment enter into the manner in which this woman was done to death', and he passed the sentence of death. But the next day he announced that in view of the jury's previous verdict and because of the fact that they had coupled a verdict of guilty of murder with a recommendation to mercy, he would pass on their recommendation to the home secretary and accompany it with their finding that the prisoner did what he did 'without premeditation of death'.

It was therefore no real surprise then that on the 19 December 1898, the reprieve from the death sentence came through, the sentence was commuted to penal servitude for life and Stoner must have considered himself very fortunate to have escaped the gallows.

9

She Committed Murder
when she was Dead

It may seem strange to find the remains of a huge abbey in what was once a remote corner of north Lincolnshire, but in the days when the roads of England were its waterways Thornton Abbey stood on a small river only a short distance from the mighty Humber itself. It was founded as a priory in 1139 for the Augustinian monks from Kirkham Priory in North Yorkshire by Sir William le Gros, Earl of Yorkshire, who was subsequently buried there. Less than ten years later it was raised to the status of an abbey. In 1264 the wooden structure of the abbey was rebuilt in stone. In 1382 Sir Thomas de Grethem, the abbot at the time, was given permission to build a gatehouse: this is the only part of the abbey which survives to this day. It is a massive structure and it is thought that the upper floors were occupied by the abbots.

Like many abbeys it has its own ghost, which is said to wander the abbey ruins late at night. It is reputed to be the ghost of Sir Thomas de Grethem, who was supposed to have fallen in love with the beautiful Heloise, the daughter of Sir William Wellam. She was a student of his and it is claimed that they were both in love, but that mattered little since her father and the rest of the church disapproved. Sir Thomas was accused of lax living. It was suggested by the dean that he dabbled in black magic, and he was put on trial and found guilty. It was reported that the punishment was proposed by the dean, but they were used to horrific punishments in those days. He was walled up alive in a secret chamber in the gatehouse. During the 1830s workmen repairing a wall discovered the room and the skeleton sitting at a desk with a book, pen and ink. The ghost who walks at night is supposed to be searching for his lost love.

Less than a mile away from the abbey and in 1933, another tragedy occurred which might well have resulted in another haunting. A spur of the main railway line from Grimsby runs north through Ulceby up to New Holland (where the ferry used to cross to Hull) and on to Barton upon Humber. Wednesday 22 November 1933 was a very dark night when William Richardson, of Lister Street in Grimsby, drove the 8.22 train from Grimsby to New Holland. He looked out of the cab frequently but could see nothing except the lights of the signals against the black background. Soon after he had left Ulceby station and as the train was slowing down approaching Thornton Abbey station he felt a bump and realised that the engine had hit something.

When the train drew into the station, driver Richardson took a lantern and got down from the engine cab. He began examining the front of the engine which was blowing clouds of white steam into the darkness. As he was doing so Stationmaster Wardle came up to him.

'What's the trouble, Bill?'

Thornton Abbey gatehouse today.

Thornton Abbey station today. The abbey gatehouse can be seen in the background.

'I think I hit something on the line. Come and look.'

Together the two men scrambled down from the platform on to the tracks and the driver held up the lantern. 'There's quite a lot of watery stuff on the wheels,' said the stationmaster. 'Could be blood I suppose.'

'Yes, there also some stuff sticking to the wheels. I obviously hit a sheep or something.'

'Looks rather a lot for a sheep. Probably a cow. It's a wonder you didn't hear it, but I suppose you wouldn't over the noise of the engine. I'll go down the line and have a look. You get a bucket of water and clean up the wheels, then you better get on to New Holland. You're late already.'

The stationmaster collected Walter Raby, a porter at the station, and together with a lantern each they began walking down the line towards Ulceby station. They had gone only about a couple of hundred yards, when Raby suddenly stopped, held his lantern high above his head and stooped down over the rails. 'Oh my God!'

'What is it?' Stationmaster Wardle came rushing up and squatted down beside his porter. They both looked down to see a woman's shoe lying by the side of the line. But it had a foot inside it. There were further nightmares to come. Next was a woman's hat. Then further on, the bottom half of a man's body was found lying between the two rails. A few feet away they came across the top half of the man and a woman's body. Both had been cut in half by the train. But the crowning horror was that beside the body of the woman was the body of a small baby.

Leaving the porter behind to watch over the bodies Wardle went back to the station. He sent someone to notify the police and then called for assistance from his other porters, most of whom lived in the village of Thornton Curtis, about a mile away and the nearest village to Thornton Abbey station. They collected canvas stretchers and by the light of lanterns carried the remains to

Looking south down the lines from Thornton Abbey station.

Thornton Abbey station gate, which Harold Mundy and Nellie Waite might have passed through.

Thornton Abbey station. The usual way on to the line was through a hand-gate onto the station platform. But nobody at the station had seen the two people on the platform. It was surmised that they could have pushed their way through a hedge to gain access to the railway lines. And thus it seemed that the tragedy was not accidental.

The inquest on the three bodies opened on the following Friday in the little waiting room at the station. There were nearly thirty people crowded into the room, including the Grimsby county coroner, Mr E. Ben Chapman, the jury, two representatives of the police and one from the railway company and reporters from the press.

The body of the man was identified by his maternal grandfather as Harold Mundy, twenty-one, a farm labourer of Thornton Curtis. The grandfather, George Howson, said that he knew that his grandson was going out with a woman called Nellie Waite, but he had never heard the boy threaten to take his own life.

Nellie Waite was only seventeen and had been employed by a Mrs Riggall, who lived in Wootton, about a mile to the south of Thornton Curtis. Nellie had been a domestic servant for the last two years. Mrs Riggall said that it was the general custom for the girl to have Wednesday evenings free and she had been in the habit of cycling over to Thornton Curtis to see her young man. She had been 'walking out with him for some time'. Mrs Riggall said that she had become suspicious of the girl's condition for some time, but when questioned, Nellie denied that there was anything the matter. But Winifred, Mrs Riggall's daughter said that Nellie had told her that she was pregnant. Nellie was usually bright, cheerful and high spirited, but of late she had seemed depressed. After she had gone out that Wednesday at about half past four in the afternoon, Mrs Riggall found in Nellie's room a note addressed to her. It told her not to wait up for her as she would not be coming back.

The main street of Thornton Curtis today, where Harold Mundy lived.

The pond in Wootton village, where Nellie Waite had worked.

Charles Waite of the Gate House, Wickenby, which is a village about half way between Market Rasen and Lincoln, said that he was Nellie's father. He had last seen his daughter on 8 or 9 October when she was at home. And she then seemed in good spirits. He had seen Harold Mundy on a number of occasions when Nellie had brought him home with her. 'I heard regularly from her every week,' he said 'and I received a letter from her yesterday. But we destroyed it to keep it from the children. It began, 'Dear Father and Mother and Brother and Sister. When you receive this letter I shall have gone out of this world into the next. Don't worry about me.' That, he said, was all he could remember of it. When he was questioned by the coroner he replied that there was no reference to Harold Mundy in the letter. And she didn't say anything about her condition. The family did not know anything about it either until they received the news of her death.

At the conclusion of the inquest the jury returned a verdict against Harold Mundy and Nellie Waite of suicide during temporary insanity. This was a device much used at the time to alleviate the stigma of suicide, which at the time was still a criminal offence. But the real surprise came with the evidence of Dr G.A. Gilmour, a GP from Barton upon Humber. He had done the post-mortem on the bodies and gave it as his opinion that their injuries were consistent with them having draped themselves across the line in the path of the train. But as the train hit Nellie her baby was born, or at least released. It was hardly touched by the impact and had in his opinion lived for a few minutes before it died.

This meant, the coroner pointed out to the jury, that because Nellie had deliberately placed herself on the railway line she had been responsible for the baby's death. And since her action was premeditated, legally she had committed murder. And the jury dutifully brought in a verdict to that effect. She remains the only woman to my knowledge who committed a murder when she was dead.

10

A Day at the Races

Wednesday morning was bright and sunny and a happy party assembled outside the public house called Tim Bobbin in Cumberland Street, which is just off Wincolmlee near the river Hull. They were members of the Tim Bobbin Recreation Club and they had been subscribing for weeks for just this very day: a day at the races. It was 8 June; the start of the Beverley Races in the year 1910.

They had hired a waggonette, drawn by four horses, and they were about to clamber aboard for the hour or so's trip to the Beverley Racecourse, when one of their number pointed to an elderly photographer who had just turned up. They all disembarked and stood grinning and grimacing in a long line in front of the waggonette, while the photographer arranged his equipment across the road. The coach driver attempted to calm the horses, which were getting restless and wanting to be off. The old man took some time to arrange his cumbersome camera stand, look through the viewfinder and place the black hood over his head, but finally he was ready. 'Watch the birdie!'

By now their smiles were becoming a little rigid, but they rallied themselves. This was going to be their day. Nothing was going to stand in the way of their enjoyment. A few ribald remarks by some caused laughter and it was a smiling group who heard the shutter click. Quickly they clambered back aboard, only to hear the anguished shout of the ancient photographer. 'I've forgotten to put the plate in the camera!'

There were more shouts and laughter. Most of them seemed to think that the old man, who was only an amateur photographer after all, was joking. But it was quite obvious they were not going to get out of the coach again. Among the passengers there were three men from the same family, Walter Henry Nozedar and his two nephews, Walter Edward Nozedar and his younger brother James William Nozedar. Edward, who was twenty-four, lived in Raywell Street, which leads into Charles Street and then into what is now Freetown Way. His wife had come, like many of the other wives, to see her husband off. He waved to her and shouted: 'My lass, if Fun wins today we shall have some fun when I get back. And don't forget to come back here tonight to meet us when we return.'

The waggonette clattered away down the cobbled street and Ruth Nozedar waved her hand. Then she turned away with all the other wives, little knowing of the tragedy which was to befall her family.

Beverley is a very ancient town. It is not known when it was first settled and built, but the collegiate church or Minster was founded in AD 126, though there have been many churches

Beverley racecourse today.

on the same site since. The present Minster was begun in 1220, though changes were made over the years and restoration work carried out 1716-69, 1825-6, and 1866-80. Another fine church is St Mary's in the centre of Beverley. Founded in 1120, it took 400 years to complete. On the outside is a plaque commemorating the death of two Danish soldiers who landed at Hull in 1689 to support Prince William of Orange when he became King of England. They had a quarrel and fought each other in a duel. One was killed and, in accordance to Danish law, the surviving soldier was beheaded.

Today Beverley's town centre is mostly occupied by houses from the Georgian and Victorian period and the market cross in the market place was erected in 1714. In the north-west corner of the town centre is a medieval arch, called the North Bar. This was one of five gateways to the town and had a drawbridge when the town was circled by a defensive ditch.

To the west of the town are the Beverley pasture lands, called Beverley Westwood, granted in perpetuity around 1380 to the people of the town. The road to York runs through them, today called the A1035, and on the north side of the road is the Beverley racecourse. It is believed that there was racing here in the sixteenth century, but the first evidence of a permanent racetrack laid out there comes from 1690. By 1910 Beverley racecourse was well established with a stand and a number of rings.

At about five o'clock on that Wednesday evening the racing had finished and people were on their way home. On the far side of the two shilling ring, up against the grandstand, three women in their early twenties were larking about. They were dressed fashionably with gaudy blouses, long skirts which trailed on the ground and large hats, but far from behaving in the normal demure fashion of ladies of the time, they were shouting at each other and their language left much to be desired. They were in fact prostitutes from Hull and they were all drunk. Bookmakers at the

Beverley market cross today.

time used low three-legged stools, both to sit on and to stand on during the racing. They could be taken apart for transporting to other racetracks and the women were engaged in dismantling the stools, but instead of stacking the legs on the grass they were throwing them at each other with much laughter and swearing.

The three Nozedar men passed close by and were rewarded with whistles and cat calls from the women. 'Now, now, my lass,' said Edward.

'Go on, go home to your mother!' shouted one of the women, who was standing on a stool.

'Put a bag over it,' replied Edward and began walking away.

'Get a pint in it,' snarled the woman, 'you ★★★★★★★!' Edward stopped and turned back. He walked towards her. 'If you say that again I'll knock you off that stool.' His face was flushed and it was apparent that he had been drinking. 'It wasn't me,' said the woman on the stool, but she got down just in case. Another of the women drew out a long hat pin from her hair and brandished it. 'If you come near me I'll run you through with this.'

By this time the shouting had attracted a crowd of onlookers. Edward's uncle and his brother tried to restrain him, but both of them looked to people standing around to be quite drunk. Then a heavily built man pushed his way through the crowd and came and stood in front of the women. He turned to Edward: 'what's the matter?'

The plaque on the outside wall of St Mary's church.

'Nothing,' said Edward sulkily.

'Then take that', and without warning he hit Edward a terrific blow on the side of the neck. The young man went down heavily and began to crawl away. The burly man, whose name was Charles Brown, followed him and bent down to grab his collar. He lifted Nozedar up to his knees and hit him again, this time in the chest. The young man rolled over on his back and his face turned blue. All this happened so quickly that nobody moved. Then the elder Nozedar came up to Brown and said, 'leave him alone!'

He was rewarded with a hard punch to the jaw and he went down. One of the women ran round and began kicking him on the ground. Young James Nozedar tried to intervene, but he too was felled by a blow from Brown. A man stepped forward from the crowd. He was Reuben Ridsdale, an honorary collector for the Hull Children's Hospital, and he had been making a collection from people at the races. 'Young man,' he said to Brown, 'clear off, don't you think you have done plenty already?'

Brown turned and swore at him. 'What's it to you?' he shouted. And approached threateningly.

'Don't hit me! I'm an older man than you. I'm only trying to give you good advice.'

A couple of the women grabbed Brown's arms and several bystanders took hold of the collector's coat and hustled him away. Brown shook off the women but pushed his way out of the crowd and stalked off. He went into the beer tent and ordered a drink.

By this time two policemen had arrived on the scene, Sgt Cunneyworth of the East Riding Police, who was stationed at Patrington, and PC Robinson, also of the East Riding Police. The sergeant took a brief look at the man lying on the ground and several men told him what had happened and where Brown had gone. He went into the beer tent, saw Brown and told him to wait until he had examined the injured man. When he looked at Nozedar again he realised that the man was either unconscious or dead and that the situation was very serious. He went back to the tent, but Brown had gone. But the PC had seen him getting into a waggonette leaving the racecourse, followed by three women.

Charles Carter, the driver, later reported that he had been waiting for fares outside the racecourse when Brown raced up, followed by three women. Brown jumped aboard shouting, 'drive on!' But Carter looking round and seeing that he had three more potential fares waited until the three women had climbed aboard. Then he whipped up the horses. But just as he did so he heard a police whistle from behind and looking round saw two policemen pelting up the road behind him. Just then Brown stood up in the cart and taking a hammer from his pocket waved it at the driver. 'Drive on or I'll murder you!' But Carter had already put on his brake. As the waggonette slid to a halt the sergeant rushed in front to grab the horses' reins and PC Robinson jumped up into the cart from behind. Brown and the three women were arrested and taken to the police station. Brown was charged with assault and the three women with riotous behaviour at the racecourse. They were lodged in the cells overnight.

Later that evening Dr George Savage of Newbegin, Beverley, was called to the police station to examine Edward Nozedar and he pronounced the man dead. The next morning Sgt Cunneyworth charged Brown with feloniously killing and slaying Walter Edward Nozedar. Brown replied, 'I never killed the man. I hit him and shoved him. There were some women there who kicked him. I was in the bar having a drink at the time.'

Later still that Wednesday evening Mrs Ruth Nozedar, who had two children, Annie, who was six, and little Edward, a year and eight months, was talking to her neighbour Mrs Lyon in a passage near her home. Both women noticed a policeman walking up the road. As they watched he stopped and asked something of a young man across the street. Mrs Lyon called across to the young man when the policeman had walked on and asked what he wanted. 'He wants a Mrs Nozedar,' he said. And Mrs Lyon realised that because Mrs Nozedar had only lived in the street a few weeks nobody knew her. The policeman was stopped and he asked Mrs Nozedar to go with him to the Norfolk Street police station.

'I suppose my husband has got himself locked up', she muttered.

Both women went to the police station, where Ruth Nozedar was told the dreadful news. 'I never saw a women change so in all my life', said Mrs Lyon afterwards. 'I thought she was going mad. She tore her hair and became almost distracted. I later went with her to his mother's place and left her there.'

Charles Brown was brought to trial at the York Assizes on 9 July 1910. He was described as a bookmaker's helper, twenty-eight, a married man living in Bar Street, Accommodation Road, Leeds. He was charged with the manslaughter of Walter Edward Nozedar and was committed for trial by the Beverley magistrates and the coroner's court.

Mr Justice Grantham was in charge of the proceedings and the prosecution was in the hands of Mr Mortimer, while Brown was defended by Mr Mellor. Mr Justice Grantham was well known for his wit in court and would often enliven the sombre proceedings with humorous observations. When one witness waving his arms about and gesticulating nearly fell out of the witness box, the judge remarked, 'that's not the first time this has happened in this court. I am expecting an action against the Corporation for manslaughter.'

The case against Brown was straightforward. Several witnesses saw him strike the first blow and all said that Nozedar had not threatened him in any way. Although Brown claimed that Nozedar had first attacked Brown's wife, she was never identified in court. The medical evidence was rather inconclusive. All Dr Savage could say for the cause of death was syncope, which is the medical term for fainting, or, he suggested, heart failure. But he stressed that it was extremely unusual for a man of twenty-four to die of syncope. It must have been brought

North Barr in Beverley today.

Norfolk Street in Hull today. The police station, where Ruth Nozedar heard the dreadful news about her husband, was situated here.

about by violence, he stated, a blow on the head, on the stomach, on the jaw or even a fall could have brought about the condition. He concluded that the man died from paralysis of the heart's action.

The judge summed up strongly against Brown. He said that if the prisoner had been charged with murder he was not at all sure that he would have been able to get out of it. There was not the slightest provocation for Brown's attacks. The jury obviously agreed with the judge and quickly brought in a verdict of guilty of manslaughter.

A police sergeant from Leeds then went into the witness box to give the prisoner's record. He said that Brown had been before the courts in Leeds twenty-eight times: nine times for felony and several times for gaming and living on the earnings of prostitutes. He had served three years penal servitude for shop breaking and eighteen months for stealing from the person. He was actually a 'ticket of leave man', which is an old term meaning that he was on parole, and had actually 235 days to go before the end of his sentence. The judge sentencing Brown said that he was a very bad man. He was only twenty-eight and all his convictions had been in the last fourteen years. He had been convicted of a range of heinous crimes although he had never been convicted before for a crime of violence. He sentenced him to five years penal servitude.

In view of Brown's record this does not seem unduly long. It was quite clear however that Brown would serve more than that since he would go back to prison to serve out his previous sentence. Of the three women arrested with Brown on the racecourse, two were convicted of riotous behaviour and served terms of imprisonment.

11

The Best Laid Schemes o' Mice an' Women

Maude Steward came from Hull. Her mother and stepfather, Mr and Mrs Bratley, lived at No. 263 Holderness Road and she was married to William Steward who was a taxi driver living in Spring Street. But she had been living apart from her husband for seven or eight years and in 1939, when she was thirty-nine, she was living at No. 176 Burgess Street, Grimsby.

Burgess Street, Grimsby, does not exist today. In 1939 it ran parallel to Victoria Street between Victoria Street and King Edward Street all the way from Pasture Street to Cleethorpe Road, passing through the Central Market. And in those days it was largely lined with back-to-back houses occupied by fishermen and their families or those who worked on the docks.

In September of that year Maude was living with a fisherman called Thomas Cossey who was forty-two and they had been living together as man and wife for about a year. Originally Cossey went to live with Maude at No. 251 Burgess Street, which was close to Lower Spring Street, near Cleethorpe Road. But in February they moved to No. 176, close to the Central Market, taking all the furniture with them. All this time Mrs Steward drew Cossey's pay as a fisherman. Little is known about Cossey, but he was described as a big handsome man and for a fisherman his brushes with the law had been remarkably few. There is no doubt that he was very much in love with Maude and wrote her long love letters. One produced in court was written from Norway.

There is also no doubt that she was not as enamoured of him as he was of her. Sometime in July when they were in a pub together, according to Cossey, another fisherman kept passing drinks across to her and she accepted them. Cossey objected to this, but he was also suspicious and when he confronted her about this other man she admitted that she had been going out with him when Cossey was at sea. She said that she would stop seeing this other man. Whether this other man was a certain John Storr we do not know. What is known is that by the end of August and the beginning of September Mrs Steward was having an affair with John Storr. Storr was a fisherman from Whitby who had come south to Grimsby looking for work. He was lodging at No. 251 Burgess Street with Arthur Steward, Maude's son, who was also a fisherman. Arthur had got married in March and had taken over No. 251, but his wife was ill and in hospital.

When the Second World War started at the beginning of September fishing virtually finished in both Hull and Grimsby. The government requisitioned most of the more modern trawlers and they became part of the Royal Naval Patrol Service. They were used for minesweeping, anti-submarine patrols and convoy duties. Many fishermen were left without work and this included

Thomas Cossey and Arthur Steward. But whereas Cossey tramped all the way to Binbrook, a matter of ten miles or so, to obtain work on a farm, Arthur stayed in Grimsby and took most of his meals at his mother's house.

On Friday 8 September Arthur, Maude and Cossey were in the little kitchen of No. 176 Burgess Street when Maude announced that her mother was ill in Hull and the next day she was going to visit her. 'Do you think you'll be coming back tomorrow night?' asked Cossey.

'I might, I don't know yet.'

'Well I'll meet the last train in, just in case you do.'

'Suit yourself.'

Cossey duly waited for the last train to come in that Saturday night at the Docks Station, which was just a few yards down from Cleethorpe Road, where the level crossing used to be. But Mrs Steward did not arrive on the train. She didn't arrive on the train because she didn't go to Hull that Saturday: instead she passed the day with her lover John Storr and spent the night with him at No. 251 Burgess Street. She didn't come back on the Sunday either and again spent the night at No. 251 with Storr. She returned on Monday to No. 176 Burgess Street, but it was plain to Cossey that something was the matter. When he returned home from work that day and saw her for the first time since Friday she would hardly speak to him. Arthur was there that

Burgess Street in the 1930s, where Maude Steward and Thomas Cossey lived. (courtesy of Grimsby library)

evening and his mother announced at about half past eight that she was going out to get some fish and chips. When she hadn't returned at half past nine Arthur left to go back to his own house. Mrs Steward returned eventually and told Cossey that she had met another man in Hull. It's likely that there was a row of some sort. But we only have Cossey's evidence of what went on and he merely said that they spoke no more about it. But it was pretty obvious that he was deeply affected by their conversation.

The next day, Tuesday, Cossey was still upset. He did not go to work and when Mrs Steward asked him why he said that it looked like rain and there was no point in going if they couldn't work outside. Arthur came round as usual for his meals. He obviously knew what was going on between Storr and his mother and the fact that they had spent Saturday night and Sunday night at his house. When asked at the committal proceedings why he hadn't told Cossey he replied that he wasn't going to tell on his mother, which under the circumstances was quite reasonable, though whether it would have affected the outcome if he had is debatable.

At some time during that day Maude asked her son if he would ask his wife if she wanted the house at No. 176 Burgess Street.

'What do you mean, come and live here?'

'Yes. You haven't got much furniture over at your place, you can have all there is here.'

Grimsby Docks station, where Thomas Cossey waited for Maude Steward. (courtesy of the *Grimsby Telegraph*)

'What are you going to do?'

'I'm going to stay with my mother in Hull for a bit. Look after her as she's not very well.'

'What about Tom Cossey?'

'He can stay with you as a lodger can't he?'

Cossey of course was present while all this was going on. It was an obvious scheme to persuade Cossey that she was going to Hull whereas as Arthur must have known or guessed she was really going to live with Storr at No. 251. Cossey believed that she was going to Hull, but since she had admitted the night before that she had met a man there he assumed she would be taking up with him. He was deeply distressed and wrote a letter that day to Mrs Steward's mother. In it he said:

I do not know whether I am on my head or my feet, but I do not mind keeping the home on for her unto you get well. But she tells me she has found somebody over there that she loves better than me. I hope she is happy with him as I love her dearly. She is the best woman in the world to me. I am broken hearted.

But during that day he went to a shop and bought two long leather boot laces.

Mrs Steward hardly spoke to Cossey all that day and in the evening she went out on her own without telling Cossey where she was going. A Mrs Cousins who knew her saw her in the

Leeds Arms public house, Victoria Street, in the 1930s, where Thomas Cossey went looking for Maude Steward. (courtesy of Grimsby library)

Coach and Horses Hotel, Cleethorpe Road. Maude came in at about 7.30 p.m. with a man Mrs Cousins didn't know, except that she knew it wasn't Cossey. But Cossey was out himself that evening, looking for her. He called at the Leeds Arms in Victoria Street, opened the side door, looked in and asked if anyone belonging to him was there. Mrs Wink, the barmaid there, realised he meant Mrs Steward and said that she hadn't seen her. He went to the Fountain Inn Vaults in Burgess Street and had a pint of beer there and from there to the Empire Hotel, Victoria Street, where he had a small whisky, which was unusual for him. All the people who saw him that night said that he looked very miserable.

During the later part of the evening Cossey came to the back gate of No. 251 and asked Arthur if he had seen his mother. Arthur said he hadn't and walked back with him to No. 176. But Cossey was restless and said he was going out again. Arthur decided to get some fish and chips and took them back to No. 176. Soon after he arrived his mother came back and shortly after that Cossey arrived.

He said to Mrs Steward, 'You're a nice one, going off and leaving me like that. I've brought you some fish. Don't you want it?'

'I don't want you running around the town looking for me. You can eat the fish.' And with that she went upstairs to bed.

Fountain Inn Vaults in Burgess Street in the 1960s. Thomas Cossey called here looking for Maude Steward. (courtesy of Grimsby library)

Arthur could see that Cossey was upset and he suggested a game of dominoes. They played on the kitchen table, but Cossey could not concentrate and eventually Arthur gave up and went back home. He was back again the next morning, but he found that the front door which led straight onto the street was locked. The garden gate in the high fence at the back, which was reached from an alley, was also locked. Arthur went back for Storr, who had spent the night at No. 251, and Storr helped Arthur to climb over the fence. Arthur then opened the back gate and the two men went into the house through a window which was not properly secured.

Immediately they could smell gas. There was no one in the bottom half of the house and so they climbed the stairs. The smell of gas was even stronger up there and the front bedroom door was closed. Arthur turned the handle and pushed, but there was something preventing the door opening. Both men put their shoulders to the door and slowly it opened. They realised that a chest of drawers had been pushed up against it. Once the bedroom door was open the smell of gas was overpowering. Through the dim light which filtered around the eiderdown which had been placed across the window as a blackout, Arthur saw Cossey. He was standing facing the wall, with his hands on the wall and his head on his hands. He was coughing. Arthur could see that the gas bracket had been broken, but he managed to get to the tap and turn it off. Then he wrenched the eiderdown from the window and jerked up the sash letting fresh air flood into the room. With the room fully lit he could now see his mother lying on the bed. He took her

Victoria Street looking towards Lock Hill (with central market on the mid-right) in the early 1900s. Arthur Steward and John Storr found a policeman here. (courtesy of Grimsby library)

by the shoulder and shook her but as his hand touched her face he felt that it was as cold as marble. He then saw that there was something tied round her neck and he realised that she was dead. He turned to John Storr. 'We'd better go and get the police.'

PC Clark of the Police War Reserve was on duty in Victoria Street when the two men approached him and he went to the house with them. Cossey was lying on the bed upstairs with his arm around Mrs Steward. When the constable shook him he said, 'why did you come so soon? Give me some more gas!' The policeman noticed that there were some cut marks on Cossey's wrists which had bled. More police arrived and Cossey was persuaded to get up. As he was being taken away he said, 'give me a knife and let me put it across my throat and let me go with her.'

He was taken to the hospital where his wounds, which were not serious, were bound up, and then he was taken to the central police station. There he was seen by DI Lamming who cautioned him and told him that the woman they had found in the house had been strangled with a boot lace and he thought Cossey was responsible.

'Yes I am. I wanted to go with her and I put one of them round my neck, but I had to take it off.'

After several remands in custody Cossey was finally brought before the magistrates on Tuesday 3 October. Mr G. Robey prosecuted on behalf of the director of prosecutions and Cossey was defended by local solicitor Walter West. Mr West was a well-known Grimsby solicitor handling criminal cases and he had helped in the defence in many high profile cases, notably the defence of Mrs Sarah Ann Hearn in 1931. He was immediately on the attack and in cross-examination of Dr A. Richmond, the police surgeon, got him to admit that people recovering from the effects of coal-gas poisoning were not responsible for what they said. And in his summing up he submitted that the Crown had not proved to the magistrates' satisfaction that a jury would convict on the evidence. The prosecution had to prove that the act was intentional and unprovoked. What had been going on between Mrs Steward and John Storr amounted to, in his submission, provocation. But the magistrates ruled against Mr West and Thomas Cossey was committed for trial on a charge of murder, at the next assizes in Lincoln.

The trial took place at the castle in Lincoln on Wednesday 1 November 1939. The prosecution was in the hands of Mr R. O'Sullivan KC and the defence was conducted by Mr A. Lyons KC. Dr J. Webster, director of the West Midlands Forensic Science Laboratory said that he and Dr Richmond performed a post-mortem examination on Mrs Steward and concluded that death was due to shock and partial asphyxia due to the application of the ligature round her neck. She actually died because her heart gave out first before asphyxia was complete.

Cossey went into the witness box to give his version of the events. He said, 'we went to bed that night. I wanted to sleep, but could not because she kept tantalising me about this other man in Hull. She said that she loved him more than me and he would be good to her. I got up and went outside rather than cause a quarrel, and walked about in the street for an hour. Then I went back to the house and upstairs. But she began to carry on to me again. She got out of bed picked up an ash tray and was going to hit me on the head with it. I lost my temper and smashed her in the face and then I don't remember anything else.'

The jury were not impressed with his story and brought in a verdict of guilty of murder, although they did add a strong recommendation to mercy. The judge put on the black cap and sentenced Thomas Cossey to death. The whole trial took only one day – quite a change from the time it takes to complete a modern murder trial.

A petition was quickly organised in Grimsby in the hope of obtaining a reprieve. It was organised by Mrs Blood, the proprietress of a café in Victoria Street where Cossey and Mrs Steward had been regular customers, and Mrs Moore, who lived next door to the scene of the crime. 'He was

The Empire public house, Victoria Street, another pub where Thomas Cossey searched for Maude Steward. (courtesy of the *Grimsby Telegraph*)

a kind, generous and cheerful man,' she said, 'I knew them both for a long time.' Mrs Blood also received a letter from Mrs Bratley, the mother of Mrs Steward, saying that she supported the petition with all her heart. The petition was even signed by Arthur Steward. In all, the petition was signed by 6,000 people.

Just a few days before he was due to be hanged the reprieve came through and Cossey was sentenced to twenty years imprisonment instead. In practice with good behaviour prisoners would then normally serve about twelve years and this in fact was what Cossey served.

In a last footnote to the case, the autopsy done on Maude Steward revealed that she was suffering from cancer of the liver. Dr Webster estimated that it was so far advanced that it would have caused her death within twelve months. So the ending of this story might have very different.

12

A Private War

.

Pocklington is about thirteen miles from York and about twenty from Hull. It is a small market town nestling at the foot of the Yorkshire Wolds on the west side of the range of hills which sweep round to reach the coast at Bridlington. Pocklington has had a long occupation. Iron Age remains have been found in the town dating back several centuries BC and before the Romans came, it was a regional centre for the Parisii, an ancient British tribe, which had links to the Continent and from which Paris gets its name. But when the Romans came they bypassed Pocklington, preferring York with its better communications, and Pocklington went into something of a decline.

The name Pocklington is thought to derive from the Old English *Poclintun* meaning the settlement (*tun*) of Pocela, who was an Angle, but the name can only be traced back as far as AD650, after the Roman period. The first Christian church was probably established by the missionary Paulinus. The Sotherby Cross in the churchyard of All Saints' church has the inscription 'Paulinus here preached and celebrated AD627'. At the end of the Viking era, the Battle of Stamford Bridge, in which King Harold of England defeated King Harold of Norway, was fought only four miles from Pocklington. But later the same year Harold was defeated by William to usher in the Norman Conquest. In medieval times Pocklington became a centre for the trading of wool, one of the main exports of the country at the time, and later its prosperity increased with the concentration of brewing and milling in the town.

Pocklington is also said to be the last place in England to hold a witch burning. In 1630 Old Wife Green was burnt at the stake in the market place for being a witch. And in 1649 thirty-two-year-old Isabella Bilington was sentenced to death at York Assizes for crucifying her mother at Pocklington. She afterwards burnt a chicken and a calf as a sacrifice. Her husband was also hanged for being an accomplice. On a more positive note, William Wilberforce wrote his first letter protesting about the slave trade while he was still at Pocklington School.

During the Second World War five airfields around Pocklington contributed valuable bomber aircraft to the assault on occupied France. In the First World War there was a battalion of the East Yorkshire Regiment stationed near Pocklington and in September 1915 a certain Pte Harry MacDonald was a cook there.

He was a strange man. For a start his name wasn't MacDonald, it was McCartney: John William McCartney. He came from Wakefield and it was there on 4 January 1899 that he married Bridget Wyles. He was twenty-four at the time. But somewhere along the line he appeared to have dumped Bridget and taken up with another young lady, Charlotte Kent, who came originally from Wednesbury, near Wolverhampton. At that time McCartney had a fruit and

All Saints' church, Pocklington. (courtesy of Ian Samuel)

fish business in Hull and he persuaded Charlotte to come and live with him. But this was not a situation which recommended itself to her. In those days living together without the benefit of marriage was not considered the respectable thing to do. So she persuaded McCartney to marry her and they were wed in July 1914, when she was twenty-eight and he was thirty-nine. He got over the embarrassment of already having a wife by simply changing his name, and so he became Henry or Harry Macdonald.

The First World War began in August 1914 and McCartney enlisted in Hull in June the following year. He was posted to one of the so called 'Chums' battalions, the 14th reserves of the East Yorkshire Regiment and sent to their camp near Pocklington. He persuaded Charlotte to come and live in Pocklington. But it is only a small town and was already full of servicemen who were billeted there, often with their wives and families. McCartney and Charlotte could not find rented accommodation and eventually had to settle for Charlotte boarding with a family while McCartney had to stay in camp. While he wasn't on duty he could come and visit Charlotte and occasionally stay the night with her.

She took up residence with William and Eliza Rodgers at No. 30 Brass Castle Hill, Pocklington, on 14 July 1915. William Rodgers was a fish fryer by trade and had a fish and chip shop a little

Market Street, Pocklington. Brass Castle Hill is the houses behind the head of the gentleman on the left of the picture. (courtesy of Andrew Sefton)

distance from the house where they lived. Relations between McCartney and Charlotte began to deteriorate as he became obsessively jealous. Pocklington was full of young soldiers, dances were held in the Assembly Rooms and there was a good opportunity for the sexes to mix and mingle. McCartney at forty may have felt that he was a little too old to compete with the much younger men and he began to suspect that Charlotte was carrying on behind his back.

He openly accused her of flirting with a Cpl Buxton at a dance and going into a darkened conservatory with him. It must be said that there was no evidence that she did anything of the kind and indeed she strongly denied the accusations when they were levelled at her. But unfortunately, denials such as these often convince a fevered imagination that there is basis for the accusations. About the middle of August on a Wednesday afternoon when he had come to Brass Castle Hill to see Charlotte a quarrel erupted into violence. He grabbed her by the throat and dragged her around the kitchen and they were only separated with difficulty by Mrs Rodgers. Afterwards he apologised and they seemed to make it up and be on good terms again. But the following Sunday it happened again. This time Mrs Rodgers was not there when it happened and only heard about it when Charlotte told her.

After she had described what happened Charlotte said, 'I'm getting frightened of him. I think maybe in one of these quarrels he might do me some harm.'

'I tell you what; I won't let him stay the night. It's my house and I can do what I like.'

'Will you tell him that?'

'I certainly will.'

And she did. McCartney seemed to take it in a reasonable fashion. He apologised to Mrs Rodgers for having caused her trouble and promised that it would not happen again. And for a while things seemed to have settled down. McCartney would come on his afternoons off and meekly depart back to the camp at night. Once or twice he did ask Mrs Rodgers rather tentatively if he could stay the night, but she was adamant that he could not and he departed peaceably. But slowly the situation began to worsen again.

On Monday 6 September McCartney arrived at Brass Castle Hill again and followed Charlotte up to her bedroom. She insisted on keeping the door open and after a while Mrs Rodgers heard shouting from upstairs. She could hear McCartney accusing Charlotte of being drunk. Mrs Rodgers rushed upstairs and heard Charlotte vehemently denying that she was, saying that she had not had a drop of anything. But it was Charlotte this time who was violent. When Mrs Rodgers entered the room she saw Charlotte land some blows to McCartney's face. Once again she got between them and separated the two.

Mrs Rodgers told Charlotte later that she ought to report her husband's behaviour to the civil or the military police. But Charlotte wouldn't, claiming that she didn't want to do anything to wreck her husband's career. The following Thursday afternoon Charlotte went up to the camp to see McCartney. She returned without him but he turned up at Brass Castle Hill at about six o'clock that night. Mrs Rodgers had asked Charlotte if she would help to fix a green blind at the fish shop and Charlotte went up to her bedroom to change her dress. McCartney followed her and Charlotte soon came running back downstairs and whispered to Mrs Rodgers that she did not want to be left alone with McCartney. Mrs Rodgers's daughter Mrs Waddington was there and she heard what Charlotte said. She offered to go with her and the two women set off for the fish shop, but they were followed there by McCartney. However, Mrs Waddington returned after a while and said that they both seemed to working together and there seemed to be no trouble between them. They returned together at nearly nine o'clock, but Charlotte took

Magistrates' court, Pocklington. The left-hand side to the rear is the police station and the right side was the court house. (courtesy of Ian Samuel)

Mrs Rodgers on one side and said. 'You won't let him stay here tonight, will you?' And Mrs Rodgers assured her that she wouldn't.

McCartney duly said that he had a pass from the camp for that night and asked if he could stay. But Mrs Rodgers said that he could not. 'Very well,' he said, 'if you can't do with me, I will get a bed somewhere else.' The three of them were in the kitchen. Mrs Rodgers was sitting at the table and the other two were standing facing each other. McCartney continued to plead with Charlotte to come and spend the night with him somewhere else. But she refused. They could both now see that McCartney was getting worked up, his face flushed and veins bulging in his neck over the tight uniform collar. Charlotte tried to defuse the situation. She said that if he went back to camp tonight tomorrow she might go away with him. But this did not satisfy McCartney. He leaned over her and took her chin in his hand. 'If you won't go back with me tonight, take that!' And he took a razor from his coat pocket and slashed her across the throat!

Charlotte collapsed on the floor grasping Mrs Rodger's knee as she went down. Then McCartney drew the razor across his own throat and he went down on his knees. Mrs Rodgers rushed out of the room shouting for help and assistance. The police were soon called and Superintendent John Robson arrived on his bicycle with Sgt Spriggs. On the grass plot opposite the Brass Castle Hill house they saw the crumpled up figure of a soldier. He was moaning and the superintendent sent Spriggs for a doctor while he went into No. 30. He found the body of Charlotte in the passage just inside the front door where she had either crawled or been dragged from the kitchen, where there was a great deal of blood. He found the razor McCartney had used on the floor in the kitchen.

Dr Angus Fairweather arrived at the house at just after eleven that night. He saw the semiconscious form of McCartney lying on the grass and examined him, then had him removed to the hospital. He could do nothing for Charlotte however and pronounced her dead at the scene.

McCartney was slow to recover from his self-inflicted wound, but eventually he was considered well enough to attend the inquest which was held in the police court in Pocklington. Charlotte's body had been taken to a stable at the Feathers Hotel. The inquest jury were sworn in at the yard of the hotel and then taken to view the body. After evidence had been presented the inquest jury brought in a verdict of wilful murder against McCartney.

McCartney went to trial at York Assizes on Wednesday 24 November 1915. The presiding judge was Mr Justice Atkin and the prosecuting counsel, Mr H. Neild, while McCartney was defended by Mr C. Paley Scott. Mr Neild outlined the case against McCartney, calling a number of witnesses – including a William Davies who was a butcher in Market Street. He said that late on Thursday night a soldier knocked on his door and asked for a drink of water, but thinking the man was drunk he refused him. Later he heard moaning and going across the road found McCartney lying on the grass severely wounded.

Superintendent Robson gave his evidence and was then cross-examined by Mr Paley Scott about McCartney's antecedents. It was obvious what line the defence would take when the superintendent admitted that McCartney had one uncle who hanged himself in 1836 and another who died in Wakefield Asylum in 1894. And another witness, Pte Newton, who was in the same company as McCartney, said that when the prisoner had been confined to barracks for seven days for some minor offence he had been brooding and sullen thereafter. But Dr Howlett the medical officer of Hull Jail said that he had been observing McCartney in prison since 15 October and he could not detect anything mentally wrong with him during that time.

Mr Paley Scott called McCartney as his only witness. McCartney gave his version of the events leading up to the crime, but on cross-examination by Mr Neild he admitted that he remembered the fitting of the green blind on the afternoon of the murder but could remember nothing of

The Feathers Hotel, Pocklington, where the jury were sworn. (courtesy of Andrew Sefton)

what subsequently occurred. The defence counsel in his speech for the defence said that the ferocity of the attack was evidence of the prisoner's insanity and he asked the jury to find that although McCartney was guilty of the crime he was insane at the time he committed it.

The judge pointed out that for a man to be judged insane he had to be thought not to know what he was doing, or if he did he did not know it was wrong. The jury had no doubts. After ten minutes they brought in a verdict of guilty of murder. The judge put on the black cap and pronounced the sentence of death.

As McCartney left the dock he moaned, 'Oh! No, no! I was mad when I did it!' But the ending of this dreadful crime was reached on Wednesday 29 December 1915, when John William McCartney was executed at Wakefield Prison.

Bibliography

BOOKS

Benjamin Bennett, *Murder Will Speak*, (Howard Timmins, 1962)

Douglas G. Browne and E.V. Tullett, *Bernard Spilsbury – His Life and Cases*, (George G. Harrap & Co. Ltd, 1951)

Francis Carlin, *Reminiscences of an Ex-Detective*, (George H. Doran, *c.* 1927)

A. A. Clarke, *The Groaning Gallows*, (Arton Books, 1994)

A.A. Clarke, *Killers at Large*, (Arton Books, 1996)

Syd Dernley with David Newman, *The Hangman's Tale*, (Robert Hale, 1989)

L. C. Douthwaite, *Mass Murder*, (John Long, 1928)

East Yorkshire Federation of Women's Institutes, *East Yorkshire Within Living Memory*, (Countryside Books and the EYFWI, 1998)

John J. Eddleston, *The Encyclopaedia of Executions*, (John Blake, 2002)

Steve Fielding, *Yorkshire Murder Casebook*, (Countryside Books, 1997)

Edward Gillett and Kenneth A. MacMahon, *A History of Hull*, (The University of Hull Press, 1989)

Ed. David Goodman, *Aspects of Hull*, (Wharncliffe Publishing, 1999)

David Goodman, *Foul Deeds & Suspicious Deaths in Hull*, (Wharncliffe Books, 2005)

Leo Grex, *Mystery Stranger than Fiction*, (Robert Hale, 1979)

Leonard Gribble, *Famous Manhunts*, (John Long, 1953)

Leonard Gribble, *Murders Most Strange*, (John Long, 1959)

Paul Harrison, *Yorkshire Murders*, (Countryside Books, 1992)

Brian Lane, *The Murder Guide to Great Britain*, (Robinson Publishing, 1993)

Martin Limon, *Tales From The East Riding*, (Tempus Publishing, 2006)

Philip Lindsay, *The Mainspring of Murder*, (John Long, 1958)

Len Markham, *Great Hull Stories*, (Fort Publishing, 2003)

John Parris, *Most of My Murders*, (Frederick Muller, 1960)

Bruce Sanders, *They Couldn't Lose the Body*, (Herbert Jenkins, 1966)

Ed. Kurt Singer, *My Strangest Case*, (W.H. Allen, 1957)

Stephen Wade, *The Wharncliffe A-Z of Yorkshire Murder*, (Wharncliffe Books, 2007)

Stephen Wade, *Yorkshire's Murderous Women*, (Wharncliffe Books, 2007)

Angus Young, *Murders of Hull*, (Hull Daily Mail, 1995)

Angus Young, *More Murders of Hull*, (Hull Daily Mail, 1995)

NEWSPAPERS

The Daily Chronicle (London)
The Daily News (London)
Grimsby Evening Telegraph
Grimsby News
Hull and North Lincolnshire Times
The Daily Mail (Hull)
Hull Daily Mail
Hull Times
Scarborough Evening News and Daily Mercury
Scarborough Post and Weekly Pictorial

MAPS

Hull Old Town 1853, (Alan Godfrey Maps 1988)
Hull (East) 1908, (Alan Godfrey Maps 2007)
Hull (NE) 1908, (Alan Godfrey Maps 2007)
Hull (West) 1908, (Alan Godfrey Maps 2006)
Hull (Hessle Road), (Alan Godfrey Maps 1999)
Kingston-upon-Hull (West) 1928, (Alan Godfrey Maps 1987)